DECISIONS AT CHATTANOOGA

DECISIONS
AT CHATTANOOGA

The Nineteen Critical Decisions
That Defined the Battle

Larry Peterson
Maps by Tim Kissel

COMMAND DECISIONS
IN AMERICA'S CIVIL WAR

The University of Tennessee Press / Knoxville

Library of Congress Cataloging-in-Publication Data

Names: Peterson, Lawrence K., author. | Kissel, Tim, cartographer.
Title: Decisions at Chattanooga : the nineteen critical decisions that defined
the battle / Larry Peterson ; maps by Tim Kissel.
Description: First edition. | Knoxville : The University of Tennessee Press, [2018] |
Series: Critical decisions in America's Civil War | Includes bibliographical
references and index. |
Identifiers: LCCN 2018011953 (print) | LCCN 2018013072 (ebook) |
ISBN 9781621904229 (kindle) | ISBN 9781621904236 (pdf) |
ISBN 9781621904212 | ISBN 9781621904212q (pbk.)
Subjects: LCSH: Chattanooga, Battle of, Chattanooga, Tenn., 1863. |
Command of troops—Case studies.
Classification: LCC E475.97 (ebook) | LCC E475.97 .P48 2018 (print) |
DDC 973.7/359—dc23
LC record available at https://lccn.loc.gov/2018011953

To my wife, Kathleen

CONTENTS

ILLUSTRATIONS

Figures

Maps

PREFACE

As many readers perhaps did, I became fascinated with the American Civil War from an early age. Initially I watched television programs about the war and read many books concerning it. My great-great-grandfather who was a Confederate brigadier general further motivated my desire to learn more. After raising a family and pursuing a career in aviation, it finally occurred to me that I should research my ancestor. This endeavor occupied many years of investigation and writing, culminating in the publication of my *Confederate Combat Commander: The Remarkable Life of Brigadier General Alfred Jefferson Vaughan Jr.*, published by the University of Tennessee Press in 2013. Vaughan fought with the Army of Tennessee in the Western Theater. I intensively researched the Army of Tennessee's lack of success, discovering, like other scholars, that its failures began with the top of the chain of command. Senior generals' antics and poor decisions resulted in many military debacles.

Newly promoted Brig. Gen. Alfred Vaughan led Vaughan's Brigade at the Battle of Chattanooga. As I examined the battle in detail, it became obvious that members of the Confederate high command made many significant blunders that contributed to their downfall. In contrast, Maj. Gen. Ulysses S. Grant made some excellent decisions leading to his victory. Certainly, a bit of luck was also involved in Grant's success.

Union forces captured not only Chattanooga but, prior to the battle, most of Tennessee. As a result, fewer goods and services were available in what Thomas Connelly calls the Confederate "Heartland." This grave blow to President Jefferson Davis and the Confederacy enabled the Union's senior commander, newly commissioned lieutenant general Ulysses S. Grant, to plan for the invasion of Georgia in 1864. The Atlanta Campaign was the result. It behooves us to examine what went right and what went wrong for both sides before and during the Battle of Chattanooga (or Missionary Ridge) on November 24–25, 1863. A series of critical decisions there helped determine the eventual fate of the Confederacy.[1]

Readers need to understand what this book is about and what it is *not* about. This is *not* another work describing the Battle of Chattanooga. Instead, this is an entirely different approach to viewing how this battle and other Civil War battles and campaigns unfolded. This is advancing to the next level of understanding a battle or campaign. As previous books in this series emphasize, this is a study of why the fighting evolved as it did, as opposed to what happened. Critical decisions, generally (but not always) made by senior commanders, directly affected the outcome of a battle. They could be made at all levels of command, from the national level to possibly the regimental one. While hundreds of important choices were made daily and even hourly, they were the result of one or more critical decisions. A critical decision is a decision of such great magnitude that after it is made, it shapes not only the events immediately following, but also the campaign or battle from that point on. I have been careful not to characterize a decision at the Battle of Chattanooga as critical when it responded to a critical decision made by someone else. This concept is key; it can be used to examine campaigns or battles in any war.

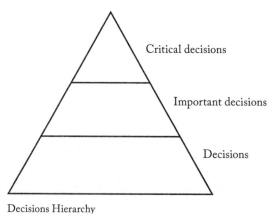

Decisions Hierarchy

To emphasize this last point, look at the Battle of Gettysburg as an example. Early on the third day of the battle, July 3, 1863, Gen. Robert E. Lee had three choices: he could attack, defend, or retreat. He decided to attack.

One of the results of that choice was the famous Pickett-Pettigrew-Trimble Charge, which was not in itself a critical decision. The reader needs to realize that crucial choices sometimes created opportunities for well-known parts of battles and campaigns to occur.

The Battle of Chattanooga's nineteen critical decisions fall into five categories and time periods:

Nine decisions shaped the battle:

1. Bragg orders a limited pursuit of Rosecrans after the Battle of Chickamauga
2. Bragg orders the establishment of poorly designated lines/positions
3. Lincoln orders the Eleventh and Twelfth Corps to Chattanooga
4. Davis decides to keep Bragg in command of the Army of Tennessee
5. Lincoln decides to consolidate the three Western Departments
6. Grant orders the "Cracker Line" opened
7. Grant orders Sherman to proceed directly to Chattanooga
8. Longstreet decides not to fortify Lookout Valley
9. Bragg decides that Longstreet will capture Knoxville

Three pre-battle critical decisions were made on November 23, 1863:

10. Grant orders Sherman to attack Bragg's right flank at Tunnel Hill
11. Grant orders Thomas to conduct a reconnaissance in force
12. Breckinridge orders Captain Green to lay out a topographical crest line of defense

Three more critical decisions were made on day one of the battle, November 24, 1863:

13. Bragg decides that Cleburne will protect the right flank at Tunnel Hill
14. Sherman decides to entrench and not attack Tunnel Hill
15. Bragg decides to abandon Lookout Mountain

Another three critical decisions were reached on day two of the fighting, November 25, 1863:

16. Sherman decides to attack with two of nine brigades
17. Grant orders Thomas to conduct a demonstration
18. Thomas's troops decide to continue the assault

One post-battle critical decision was made on November 27, 1863:

19. Bragg orders Cleburne to protect the
    Confederate retreat

Critical decisions relate to strategy, tactics, operations, organization, logistics, and personnel. Each critical decision is examined in the same manner. After the situation is presented, options for the decision-maker are discussed, followed by the option selected by (usually) a commander. At this point, the critical decision's outcome is evaluated. Discussion of the options not chosen then takes place, in some cases leading to interesting speculation about alternative battle scenarios. Hopefully, this format will entice readers to carry out their own investigations as to how the Battle of Chattanooga might have unfolded differently.

It is always beneficial to visit locations where critical decisions were made in order to gain a better perspective. Appendix I is a driving tour of where many of the critical decisions of the Chattanooga Campaign were made in order to enhance the reader's appreciation and understanding of terrain and other significant features. Quotes from some of those records pertinent to the critical decisions are included. Appendix II and III are the respective Union and Confederate Orders of Battle, which are included for the reader's convenience.

Please note that Union army corps were, contrary to most Civil War books, not designated by Roman Numerals until after the war. Therefore, the corps numbers are spelled out. Also the abbreviations of officers' ranks utilized by the armies were different than today. The best example is lieutenant colonel, which was abbreviated "Lieut. Col." during the war. Later it became "Lt. Col.," and today it is "LTC." Thus, readers will see "Lieut. Col." and other abbreviations peculiar to the war used throughout this work.

I would like to acknowledge the help and support provided by many individuals. Leading the way was Chickamauga and Chattanooga National Military Park historian James Ogden III. Many conversations and emails with Jim helped steer me clear of some mistakes and his counseling is most appreciated. Also at the park, ranger Lee White provided as a reader many insightful comments and suggestions. The Chickamauga expert Doctor William Glenn Robertson provided many necessary and helpful corrections and advice as another reader.

Special thanks goes to my very good friend Matt Spruill who founded this series and asked me to assist him with it. His vast experience and knowledge has kept me on track over the years with my many writing endeavors.

I wish to express my appreciation for all of the help, guidance, and support provided by the University of Tennessee Press. The guidance of director Scot Danforth and the partnership of acquisitions editor Thomas Wells made this book possible. Copy editor Elizabeth Crowder somehow managed to make my manuscript readable. Also thanks to Jon Boggs, Stephanie Thompson, Linsey Perry, Tom Post, and the rest of the staff for their efforts on my behalf.

Through the American Battlefield Trust I have been able to meet and correspond with many historians of the war. I strongly encourage anyone with an interest in the Civil War to join and support President James Lighthizer and the Trust's efforts to preserve the battlefields (www.battlefields.org). The excellent maps provided by Tim Kissel greatly enhance the readers' understanding of the various aspects of the battle. Thanks, Tim.

Finally, I would like to express thanks to my wife Kathleen who has patiently told me for years that she knows who won the war. Her bucket list probably did not originally include Chickamauga, Chattanooga, and many other Civil War sites. Her support has been critical to my efforts.

Larry Peterson
Evergreen, Colorado

INTRODUCTION

In the Eastern Theater the first major battle of the war was the Union defeat at First Bull Run (or First Manassas) in July 1861. After this initial engagement both sides regrouped and rebuilt their respective armies. In March 1862 Maj. Gen. George B. McClellan moved the large Union Army of the Potomac by ship to Fort Monroe, and then up the Virginia Peninsula toward the Confederate capital at Richmond. In late June and early July Gen. Robert E. Lee, now commanding the Army of Northern Virginia, commenced the Seven Days Battles, which ended in Union retreat. After initial success at the Second Battle of Manassas in late August 1862, Lee invaded Maryland in the late summer. This maneuver brought about the bloody Battle of Antietam and Confederate retreat. After Confederate victories in the Eastern Theater at Fredericksburg and Chancellorsville in December 1862 and May 1863, Confederate fortunes suffered a series of setbacks. The repulse of Lee's Army of Northern Virginia at Gettysburg in early July 1863 dashed Southern hopes of immediate victory and resulted in the loss of thousands of irreplaceable soldiers. Confederate fortunes suffered likewise in the Western Theater.

At the beginning of the Civil War in the Western Theater, little-known brigadier general Ulysses S. Grant advanced down the Mississippi River and fought the small Battle of Belmont in November 1861. Grant followed up with victories at Forts Henry and Donelson in February 1862. The Tennessee and Cumberland Rivers were consequently opened as Union routes of invasion, leading to the Union victory at the Battle of Shiloh near Corinth, Mississippi, in April.

After the Battle of Shiloh, Gen. Braxton Bragg replaced Gen. P. G. T. Beauregard as commander of the Army of the Mississippi, which would soon be renamed the Army of Tennessee. Bragg then led his army into Tennessee and Kentucky in the Kentucky Campaign of 1862. Conducted jointly with Maj. Gen. Edmund Kirby Smith's small Army of Kentucky, augmented by a division from Bragg's army, this invasion was initially successful. While Bragg moved north from Chattanooga and advanced into Kentucky, Kirby Smith advanced north from Knoxville. On August 30, 1862, Kirby Smith soundly defeated a Union army commanded by Maj. Gen. William "Bull" Nelson at Richmond, Kentucky. This was perhaps the most one-sided victory of the Civil War. After the two commands joined, Bragg went so far as to "inaugurate" a Confederate governor of Kentucky in Frankfort, the capital. At the Battle of Perryville on October 8, Bragg's one corps fought Maj. Gen. Don Carlos Buell's three corps of the Army of the Ohio. A natural phenomenon called acoustic shadow kept Buell's headquarters from hearing the battle; this was why only one Union corps was actually engaged. While Bragg won the day, he quickly realized that he was outmanned and retreated.

Bragg's reasons for retreating were many. The male citizens of Kentucky were not flocking to his army to enlist for the Confederate cause. Moreover, supplies and ammunition for his army were dwindling. Bragg could not reasonably maintain the extremely long line of supply necessary for his troops' existence, and projected reinforcements from the small armies commanded by Gens. Sterling Price and Earl Van Dorn were not going to materialize. Thus Bragg ordered a withdrawal from Kentucky. In doing so, he incensed many of his officers and men and planted seeds of dissension within his army, especially among some of the higher-ranking brass. This withdrawal was conducted under extreme drought conditions, and it caused great hardship for officers and soldiers alike. Upon Bragg's return to Knoxville, he was ordered to Richmond to explain his conduct during the campaign. He positioned his newly named Army of Tennessee in winter quarters south of Nashville.

When Buell failed to pursue Bragg and Kirby Smith during their retreat from Kentucky, Lincoln replaced him with Maj. Gen. William S. Rosecrans. Rosecrans was ordered to attack Bragg despite the winter season, and after much preparation he advanced on the Confederate general at Murfreesboro. Bragg quickly concentrated his forces near the city. The horrific Battle of Stones River took place from December 31 to January 2, resulting in the seventh-bloodiest engagement of the Civil War. The outcome was a Confederate retreat and Union occupation of Murfreesboro. Both sides prepared to commence fighting in the spring, when the roads would likely be dry enough to permit operations.

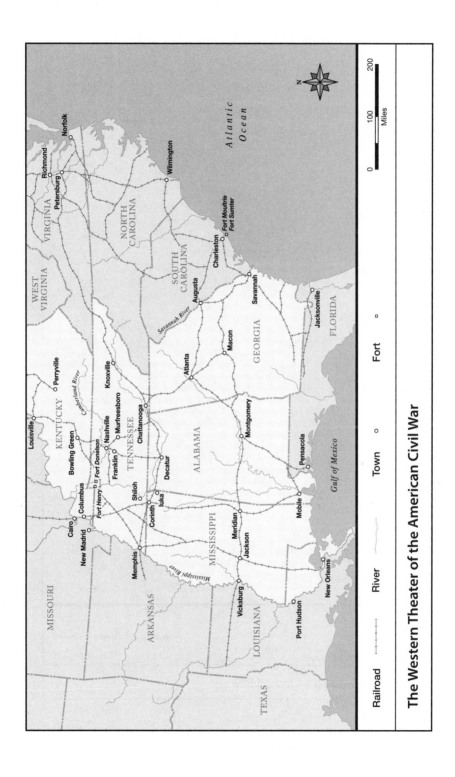

The Western Theater of the American Civil War

Railroad   River   Town ○   Fort □

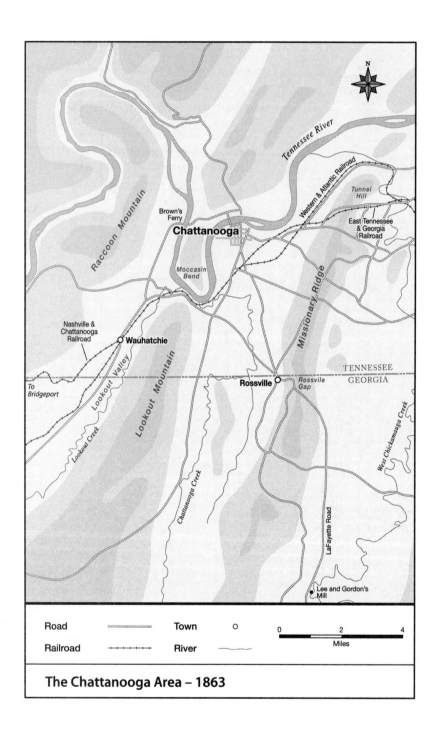

The Chattanooga Area – 1863

Meanwhile, Major General Grant had begun operations to capture Vicksburg, the last Confederate bastion on the Mississippi River. After months of failures, Grant finally captured the city after a siege on July 4, 1863, which was in concert with the Rebel loss at the Battle of Gettysburg. During these twin losses by the Confederacy, the successful advance of Rosecrans's Army of the Cumberland during the Tullahoma Campaign was often overlooked. A methodical general, Rosecrans prepared to go on the offensive in Middle Tennessee. At the same time, Bragg allowed his army to remain spread out over miles to obtain supplies and good grazing. Rosecrans launched his Tullahoma Campaign on June 23, and in eleven days he had brilliantly outflanked Bragg's army, forcing its withdrawal to Chattanooga.

Following this remarkable operation with insignificant loss of life to the Union, Rosecrans began the Chickamauga Campaign. After Rosecrans sent his three corps toward Chattanooga and other points south, Bragg abandoned the city and planned to attack Rosecrans's units individually. However, wide mistrust had developed within the Army of Tennessee. Bragg's sound plan of attacking part of Maj. Gen. George H. Thomas's corps advancing into McLemore's Cove (valley) failed to materialize. Realizing the vulnerability of his dispersed corps, Rosecrans ordered them all, including his reserve corps, to concentrate south of Chattanooga. Bragg's resolve to cut Rosecrans's supply line to Chattanooga set the stage for the Battle of Chickamauga, the largest battle in the Western Theater.

While Rosecrans united his corps to protect his supply line to Chattanooga, Bragg marshalled his corps and ordered an attack on the Union forces located around Lee and Gordon's Mill and points north along the La Fayette Road. Initial contact and fighting began on September 18, 1863. Vicious combat erupted the next day, and though there was no clear winner, both sides sustained thousands of casualties. Though he likely did so for personal advancement and the chance to command Bragg's army, Lieut. Gen. James Longstreet, Gen. Robert E. Lee's senior corps commander and right-hand man, had petitioned the Confederate government to allow his corps to go west and help the Army of Tennessee face Rosecrans. This movement was eventually approved. Via a roundabout series of railroad connections (the direct route through Chattanooga was under Union control), two of Longstreet's three divisions (Maj. Gen. George Pickett's division had been decimated at the Battle of Gettysburg) and Col. E. Porter Alexander's artillery battalion were transported south to Atlanta and then north to Catoosa Station, just south of Ringgold, Georgia, near the battlefield. Longstreet arrived at Catoosa Station on the afternoon of the nineteenth. He slowly made his way to

Bragg's headquarters, arriving close to midnight. Aware of Longstreet's impending arrival, Bragg reallocated his command into two wings commanded by Lieut. Gens. James Longstreet and Leonidas Polk.

After Polk's failure to commence an attack at dawn on the twentieth as ordered, Confederate luck seemingly changed for the better. Longstreet lined up his wing, somewhat by accident, while waiting for the battle to commence. Three divisions were placed one behind another in his center, and a division on each flank augmented them. Finally ordering the attack at about 11:30 a.m., Longstreet and his wing struck an opening in the enemy's line. Rosecrans had unnecessarily ordered Brig. Gen. Thomas J. Woods's division to pull out of the Union front line and support another division. Attacking through and on both sides of the gap left by Wood's division, Longstreet's men quickly routed the right of the Union line. Continued combat led to a final resistance cobbled together by Major General Thomas on Snodgrass Hill, while Rosecrans eventually fled to Chattanooga. After holding off the Confederates' piecemeal attacks during the afternoon, and receiving last-minute support from Rosecrans's Reserve Corps under Maj. Gen. Gordon Granger, Thomas ordered those left fighting to retreat back to Rossville. From Rossville, the troops eventually withdrew to Chattanooga. Although some thirty-four thousand casualties were suffered by both sides, the Confederate Army of Tennessee had finally emerged victorious. This would remain that army's only victory of the Civil War.

As will be discussed, Bragg did not fully capitalize on this victory. He initially refused to order the pursuit of Rosecrans; much of his force was simply too exhausted and depleted for the maneuver. By the time a pursuit was ordered, Union soldiers had regrouped in strength in and surrounding Rossville Gap on September 21. By the twenty-second, Northern soldiers had successfully retreated into Chattanooga proper and were continuing to erect strong entrenchments around it. Bragg realized that a direct attack on the Union position was not feasible, and he was essentially forced to conduct a siege and attempt to block the Union line of supply. The Confederate victory had become a hollow one indeed.

CHAPTER 1

SHAPING THE CAMPAIGN

If you have bypassed the preface, please direct your attention there and read the definition of *critical decision* to more fully understand the presentations in this book.

Prior to the Battle of Chattanooga, nine critical decisions shaped the upcoming fighting on both sides. Grant was appointed overall commander of the Union forces at Chattanooga, and he both ordered and was given reinforcements. He ordered his supply line to be reinstated and prepared to fight his way out of Chattanooga. Bragg failed to follow up his victory at Chickamauga but remained in command. He was careless with his siege lines, and he depleted his command by sending Lieutenant General Longstreet's divisions to capture Knoxville. As Grant built up his forces, Bragg reduced his.

Bragg Orders a Limited Pursuit of Rosecrans After the Battle of Chickamauga

Situation

Because of the sequence of the Battles of Chickamauga and Chattanooga, this critical decision occurred at the end of the fighting at Chickamauga. However, this choice would impact the course of events for all soldiers during the coming months and the Battle of Chattanooga.

General Braxton Bragg, CSA. The Photographic History of the Civil War, Vol. 10, 243.

The Battle of Chickamauga occurred between September 18 and 20, 1863.
Combat concentrated south of Chattanooga, Tennessee—a section of north-
ern Georgia between West Chickamauga Creek and east and west of the
La Fayette Road that ran from Chattanooga to La Fayette, Georgia. Gen.
Braxton Bragg attempted to place his Army of Tennessee between Maj.
Gen. William S. Rosecrans's Army of the Cumberland and his supply base at
Chattanooga. While the battle began with limited fighting on September 18,
the fighting on the nineteenth was horrific but inconclusive. During the night
the Yankees fortified their lines, piling up rocks, fence logs, and rails. Thus
they were prepared for attacks by the Rebels on the twentieth.[1]

Earlier in the year, Lieut. Gen. James Longstreet had proposed to the
Confederate government that he and his corps of Gen. Robert E. Lee's Army
of Northern Virginia be transferred to assist with operations in the Western
Theater. Longstreet's real desire was to obtain command of Bragg's army, and
soon after his arrival he would become problematic for the general. After the
Battle of Gettysburg, Longstreet's request was granted. He and his divisions,
commanded by Maj. Gen. Lafayette McLaws and Brig. Gen. Micah Jenkins
(Maj. Gen. George Pickett's division was too mauled after the Battle of Gettysburg to go west), traveled by train from Richmond to Atlanta. The troops
then journeyed north to Catoosa Station, just south of Ringgold. Longstreet's

men began arriving on September 18, and some of them participated in the fighting near Reed's Bridge. Longstreet himself arrived on the nineteenth, reporting to Bragg near midnight. Bragg, anticipating Longstreet's arrival, had restructured his army into two wings. Longstreet was in charge of the left wing, which he organized early on the twentieth. He lined it up into a column of divisions and made it a formidable attacking force.[2]

On the Union side, the sleep-deprived Rosecrans was obviously concerned about his tactical situation. He ordered several divisions to reinforce Maj. Gen. George H. Thomas, who commanded the left flank of the Union army. Inadvertently, Rosecrans ordered a division to vacate a segment of his otherwise strong line and fill in for a division that he believed was absent. The unit in question was supposed to have moved, but last-minute circumstances had delayed that change. Rosecrans ordered Maj. Gen. Thomas J. Wood to pull out of his position in line and fill the supposed gap. Wood knew Rosecrans was mistaken. Yet with the concurrence of his division commander, Wood nonetheless withdrew his division, creating a huge breach in the Union line. Coincidentally, Longstreet had lined up his attacking force at this opening. Longstreet gave the order to advance, and his troops moved directly into the gap left by Wood. They also attacked the Union soldiers on both sides, which allowed the Rebels to quickly breach the Union line. Only Thomas's delaying action on Snodgrass Hill, aided by the last-minute arrival of two reserve brigades from Maj. Gen. Gordon Granger's Reserve Corps, prevented a total rout. For his performance, Thomas won the sobriquet "Rock of Chickamauga." Awakening early on September 21, Longstreet's men expected another day of combat. They were somewhat astonished to discover no Yankees on the battlefield.[3]

After the fighting on Snodgrass Hill, the Yankees retreated to Rossville Gap, strongly fortifying it and the adjacent areas of Missionary Ridge. Union forces were well situated to defend the gap. However, they were subject to being outflanked by the Rebel commands inevitably in pursuit. Although driven off the battlefield by assaults all afternoon, the Federal position was strong and morale was high. Of course, the Rebel high command was unaware of these facts.[4]

Options

After winning the Battle of Chickamauga, Bragg had two options, both of which included protecting his supply line, the Western and Atlantic Railroad. He could pursue Rosecrans's army as it retreated back to Chattanooga. Alternatively, he could regroup and refit before advancing toward Chattanooga to face Rosecrans's men.[5]

Option 1

Bragg's first option was to pursue Rosecrans's routed army, potentially seizing more of its soldiers and equipage and forcing it to retreat farther. By recapturing Chattanooga he might be able to hold off any Union invasion south of that city for the foreseeable future. Perhaps most importantly, direct railroad transportation to the East Coast could be reestablished. However, retaking Chattanooga would likely result in further loss of life for Bragg's exhausted, worn-down soldiers. He lacked sufficient horses and wagons to supply his army in the field, away from the railroad.[6]

Option 2

Bragg could decide not to pursue Rosecrans's retreating army. The Confederates' exhaustion would hinder an immediate pursuit, as would the need to minister to the wounded, bury the dead, and collect arms and ammunition lying about the battlefield. Bragg never had enough horses and supply wagons. Additionally, his army had been augmented by the arrival of Longstreet's divisions, which did not bring any supporting units. This lack of pursuit would allow the Yankees to retreat, erect fortifications, and await a possible Rebel attack. Certainly, parts of Bragg's army were incapable of giving chase. Yet other portions of his army, including forces from Maj. Gen. Benjamin F. Cheatham's division and Brig. Gen. Nathan B. Forrest's cavalry, were reasonably fresh and available.[7]

Decision

Bragg made the critical decision to cautiously pursue Rosecrans's retreating army.[8]

Results/Impact

Bragg finally initiated a limited pursuit of Rosecrans, whose men had initially entrenched in and around Rossville Gap. The Union army was allowed not only to make its way into Chattanooga, but also to quickly erect protective fortifications around the city. By this time in the Civil War, soldiers recognized that it was usually fruitless to charge such fortifications with any expectation of victory. Bragg quickly realized that he was unlikely to break through these Union entrenchments. He also knew that if he did, the cost in Confederate casualties would be unacceptable. Bragg's limited pursuit forced him to choose an alternative plan. He could launch a maneuver to draw Rosecrans out of Chattanooga, or he could lay a semi siege (he did not have enough soldiers to completely surround the city) in hopes of starving out his opponents. Geography also played an important role in Bragg's choice.

Realizing the difficulty of maintaining a supply line while maneuvering his army, he quickly established a siege line around parts of Chattanooga. By fortifying Missionary Ridge, Lookout Mountain, and Lookout Valley, Bragg effectively locked Rosecrans's army into the city.[9]

Parts of Bragg's army did not see active combat on September 20, and they could have been assigned pursuit operations. More importantly, an aggressive pursuit through McFarland's Gap might well have allowed a significant Rebel presence into Lookout Valley. These troops could have ensured a faster shutdown of supplies into Chattanooga for Rosecrans's army.[10]

Bragg's pursuit of Rosecrans after Chickamauga was noteworthy for its initial lack of aggressiveness. This approach resulted in the events leading to the battles for Chattanooga, and in the ultimate Confederate rout and loss of that city and its critical railroad center. Chattanooga's fate contributed to the demise of the Confederacy with Maj. Gen. William T. Sherman's successful Atlanta Campaign, March to the Sea, and movement to join Lieut. Gen. Ulysses S. Grant and the Army of the Potomac at Petersburg.[11]

Alternative Decision and Scenario

A more aggressive pursuit of Rosecrans's army by at least portions of Bragg's army might have resulted in the capture of additional Yankee prisoners and equipage. More importantly, the Rebels' capture of Lookout Valley and total elimination of supply routes to Middle Tennessee could have forced Rosecrans to abandon Chattanooga. This result would have been even more beneficial to the Confederacy. It would have allowed the reopening of railroad transportation to and from Chattanooga, as well as the repositioning of Bragg's army to regain Middle Tennessee. Such outcomes could have made the Battle of Chickamauga a truly significant first victory for the Army of Tennessee. They would also have reassured the Confederacy that it could still win in the Western Theater. Furthermore, these results would have delayed or even eliminated the Atlanta Campaign of 1864, which contributed to President Abraham Lincoln's reelection in November of that year. Many Confederates hoped that Lincoln's replacement by a less hawkish president might lead to a cease-fire and the eventual recognition of the Confederacy as a separate nation.[12]

Bragg Orders the Establishment of Poorly Designated Lines/Positions

Situation

Upon finally advancing to Chattanooga on September 23, Gen. Braxton Bragg and his men found the Union Army of the Cumberland already secure within both new and old entrenchments. Improvements to the works were also underway. Bragg quickly realized that, even though largely surrounded, the Union forces before him gave no indication they were about to retreat. Further, it now appeared that an attack on these new Union works would have little chance of success. Bragg quickly decided to surround much of the Union position near and inside Chattanooga with a siege line, and he ordered defensive lines established. As noted above, Bragg did not have enough soldiers to completely encircle Chattanooga, in part due to the complicated terrain.[13]

Options

It was quickly obvious to Bragg that he needed to protect his left flank on Lookout Mountain and in Lookout Valley. Yet he had three options to consider when placing his defensive lines along Missionary Ridge. Bragg could station troops on the ridge's crest, at its bottom, or in both locations.[14]

Option 1

Missionary Ridge had the potential to be an impregnable defensive position. Rising some six hundred feet above the valley floor, its terrain gave defenders a tremendous advantage. Any force attempting to assault the ridge when it was properly manned faced direct and enfilading fire from both infantry and artillery. It was generally accepted that the ridge was simply too strong to attack; the chance of success was almost nil. Like most of his army, Bragg believed it unlikely that a position on Missionary Ridge would be attacked. The option of a line of Confederates atop the ridge would be sufficient to discourage a Union assault.[15]

Option 2

Logically, Bragg could order a defensive line to be established at the base of Missionary Ridge. A picket line could be placed well in advance of these troops. This arrangement would provide Bragg with near-instant knowledge of any Union advance out of Chattanooga toward the ridge or southward. Bragg could use distance between his line at the bottom of the ridge and the Union line behind fortifications in Chattanooga as a defensive buffer.[16]

Option 3

Bragg also had the option of establishing lines at the top and bottom of Missionary Ridge. Initially, this plan appeared to take advantage of both positions. The downside to this choice was that it spread out the limited Rebels available.[17]

Decision

Bragg selected Option 2, placing a defensive line at the bottom of Missionary Ridge and a picket line well in advance of it, running through Orchard Knob. This was a logical choice to keep Rosecrans's army hemmed in behind its Chattanooga fortifications. The defensive line at the base of Missionary Ridge consisted of a series of rifle pits and other earthworks. Although both sides believed Bragg had established a defensive line atop Missionary Ridge, this opinion was technically inaccurate. The soldiers positioned there were not ordered to establish a defensive line until November 23 (this disposition will be discussed with a later critical decision).[18]

Results/Impact

Since the Union defensive line was near the edge of Chattanooga, much open ground remained between it and the base of Missionary Ridge. Therefore Bragg, who was on the offensive, established a picket line hundreds of yards forward from the ridge's foot. Rifle pits and entrenchments stood behind this line. Along part of the ridge, Bragg also established a second defensive line about halfway up the slope. Initially, these would appear to be good defensive measures. But, as the situation changed from a Rebel advance on Chattanooga to a siege, these deployments became problematic and eventually disastrous for Bragg and his men.[19]

Chronologically, these lines were established beginning September 23. The errors concerning their location were not fully evident until November 25, when Maj. Gen. George Thomas's Army of the Cumberland (Thomas had replaced Rosecrans) launched its diversionary assault on the base of Missionary Ridge. Apparently, Bragg considered a direct attack on Missionary Ridge so unlikely that he did not seriously evaluate the consequences of these lines' placement. In fact, he spent much of his time dismissing or reshuffling his commanders in retaliation for doubting his ability.[20]

The commanders of the troops at the base of Missionary Ridge issued vague or conflicting instructions that seriously complicated the issue. Some soldiers were ordered to hold these entrenchments at all costs. Others were told to retreat up the slopes if their men were about to be overrun. These instructions caused obvious confusion for the Confederates during Thomas's demonstration on November 25. Moreover, they contributed significantly to the Confederate loss of Chattanooga.[21]

The disposition of pickets was a logical and necessary requirement to provide warning of an enemy attack. However, placing rifle pits and entrenchments at the base of Missionary Ridge doomed some soldiers. Unless they

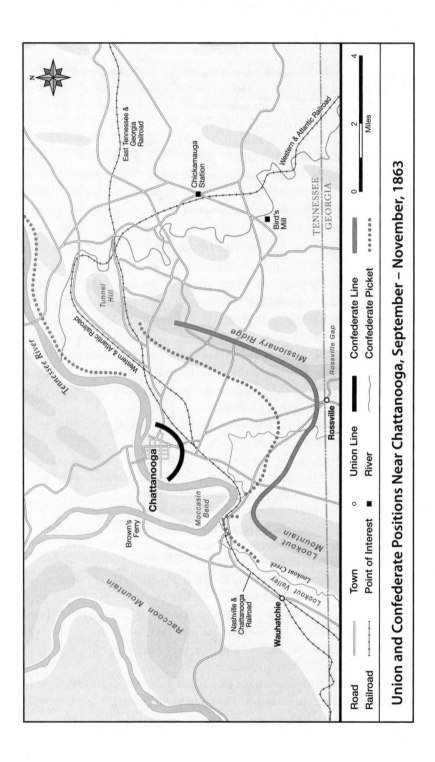

Union and Confederate Positions Near Chattanooga, September – November, 1863

were designated the sole defensive line and fully manned, these fortifications became a series of traps for the Rebel soldiers assigned to them if a large Union force attacked. As these men would discover, their only options in the event of an assault—if they were not killed or wounded—were surrendering or attempting to retreat up the steep slopes of Missionary Ridge. Once Bragg decided that he had no choice but to go on the defensive and maintain a siege, he should have reassessed the value of the aforementioned entrenchments. He no longer needed pickets at the base of the ridge; any Union activity was immediately visible from its top. Moreover, a defensive line on top of the ridge would naturally be much stronger.[22]

Alternate Decision and Scenario

Bragg's other option was to strongly fortify Missionary Ridge. Coupled with a strong line of fortifications, the ridge's natural defensive terrain would present an almost impregnable defense. As will be noted in discussion of another critical decision, "Breckinridge Orders Captain Green to Lay Out a Topographical Crest Line of Defense," military doctrine would have required Bragg to fortify the crest of Missionary Ridge. Though it appeared very unlikely that any army would assault the ridge, that contingency should nevertheless have been anticipated.[23]

Bragg was initially correct in ordering a picket line established forward of Missionary Ridge's base while he probed the Union defenses. His positioning rifle pits and entrenchments at the base of the ridge was likewise a useful deployment of troops. However, when Bragg transitioned from offensive operations to a siege, he should have reconsidered the placement of these forces. A small picket line would have provided some early notification of a Union attack. However, Confederates atop Missionary Ridge could easily have discerned such movements. By ordering his men at the bottom of the ridge to its crest, and by making the crest into a strong defensive line, Bragg would have garnered two significant advantages. First, he would not have lost many of his soldiers at the bottom of the ridge. Perhaps more importantly, these men's escape up the ridge would not have been necessary. This circumstance would have precluded the requirement that Rebels at the crest not shoot; they feared causing casualties among their own. If the crest of the ridge had been properly defended, including the addition of the men previously at its base, the November 25 assault would have met with much stronger resistance from the beginning. The Union assault may still have been effective. However, its odds of success would have been considerably reduced. Bragg apparently considered his occupation of Missionary Ridge so impregnable that he did

President Abraham Lincoln, USA. Library of Congress.

not think it was necessary to fortify this line. On November 23 and 25 the results of this decision would become critical.[24]

Lincoln Orders the Eleventh and Twelfth Corps to Chattanooga

Situation

At about 4:00 p.m. on September 20 President Abraham Lincoln and Secretary of War Edwin Stanton received the first news of the disaster at Chickamauga from Assistant Secretary of War Charles A. Dana. Dana had been assigned to observe the battle for Edwin Stanton and the War Department. These bad tidings were followed by a message from Major General Rosecrans confirming Lincoln and Stanton's worst fears—a sound Union defeat had indeed occurred. The president and secretary of war were naturally distressed by the news, and they immediately began contemplating future movements by both sides. After receiving another report from Dana that Rosecrans was preparing to defend Chattanooga, Stanton and Secretary of the Treasury Salmon P. Chase pressured Lincoln and his chief of staff, Maj. Gen. Henry Halleck, to provide reinforcements.[25]

Options

In order to confront this disaster, Lincoln had two options: order whatever assistance Rosecrans considered exigent, or send help in the form of additional manpower.[26]

Option 1

A very logical option for Lincoln was providing Rosecrans any military resources he deemed necessary to recover from his recent defeat. Who better knew what was needed than the commander on scene? Although unlikely, attempting to anticipate Rosecrans's requirements might be counterproductive.[27]

Option 2

Lincoln's other option was to immediately send Rosecrans reinforcements on the assumption that they would be of value. The size of the supporting forces could vary from a division to several corps. But Rosecrans would surely welcome any additional men. As it would take weeks for them to arrive at Chattanooga, the sooner these reinforcements were ordered to join Rosecrans, the sooner they would be of service to him. Extra soldiers would need to be supplied with food, fodder, and proper ammunition prior to and during their movement, as well as upon their arrival. At this time Rosecrans could not adequately supply his current force, much less additional men. Supplying troops for the transfer would reduce the Army of the Potomac's manpower advantage.[28]

Decision

It took Stanton and Chase until September 23 to overcome Lincoln's objection to removing troops from near Washington, DC. Yet Lincoln was finally convinced to allow the movement, and he made the critical decision to provide immediate help. At 2:30 a.m. on September 24, the Eleventh and Twelfth Corps (roman numeral corps designation did not occur until after the Civil War), stationed in Virginia near Washington, DC, were ordered to amass five days' rations and head to Chattanooga. These two corps consisted of some twenty-three thousand soldiers under the command of Maj. Gen. Joseph "Fighting Joe" Hooker. The Union defeat at the Battle of Chancellorsville occurred under Hooker's command. Fighting Joe had since been relieved of command of the Army of the Potomac, and he was looking for a way to redeem himself. Here was such an opportunity. While Lincoln was skeptical that Hooker's force would reach Chattanooga in time, the movement began nonetheless.[29]

Results/Impact

It was over a month before these reinforcements arrived in the Chattanooga area. The Eleventh and Twelfth Corps were one more force augmenting the Union command in Chattanooga, and they would play key roles in the fighting as the Federals battled their way out of the siege.[30]

As noted above, Bragg's agenda was purging his army of personal enemies. He accomplished this goal in part by ordering them away on assignments. In particular, Bragg sent Longstreet, who had become simply too critical of him, off to Knoxville (discussed later). The loss of Longstreet's Corps reduced Bragg's available manpower considerably. Further assignments of brigades and divisions to Knoxville reduced the number of men available to resist the Federals at Chattanooga. The addition of Hooker's two corps would eventually provide Grant with a sizable advantage in the number of soldiers available for breakout operations.[31]

At that time and for some time to follow, the inadequate Union supply line was an important consideration with the dispatch of reinforcements to Chattanooga. Feeding additional men would further exacerbate a severely strained situation. The existing Northern supply line could not adequately meet the minimum requirements for food, feed, ammunition, and other necessities to resupply and rebuild the Army of the Cumberland. It was fortuitous that Grant followed-through on Rosecrans' initializing the opening of the "Cracker Line" (another upcoming critical decision) once he was appointed to overall command. Hooker and his men were able to stabilize the route through Lookout Valley. Had Hooker and his corps not been dispatched and not arrived when they did, it likely would have taken several more weeks for Sherman's Army of the Tennessee to reestablish the "Cracker Line." Grant's battle plan would then have been delayed. His Army of the Cumberland would have suffered even more and taken longer to recover and increase its supplies. Thus the timing of Hooker's arrival was excellent![32]

Under Hooker's new and different command of three divisions at the beginning of the battle, one from each army emboldened him to carry out the successful attack on Lookout Mountain. While this action did not ensure Grant's victory at Chattanooga, it was certainly of some value. Hooker's other forces assisting Sherman were at least of psychological importance to the Union effort. These reinforcements proved invaluable when the final battle began.[33]

Alternate Decision and Scenario

What might have resulted had Lincoln not sent reinforcements to Chattanooga? Now in command, Grant might well have attempted his breakout

President Jefferson Davis, CSA. Library of Congress.

plan without Hooker and his two corps. The strategy would have been less likely to succeed. But Grant could still have managed to ensure Chattanooga's relief. With either Rosecrans early on, or with Grant in command, either one might have quickly requested support to rebuild the Army of the Cumberland and improve their chances of breaking Bragg's siege. Thus Lincoln's approval of reinforcements allowed these divisions to begin the journey to Chattanooga that much sooner.[34] Grant's Army of the Cumberland likely would have suffered even more and taken longer to recuperate and increase its provisions. Hooker's arrival and his men's participation in the Battle of Wauhatchie would not have occurred, seriously compromising Grant's efforts to open the "Cracker Line."[35]

Davis Decides to Keep Bragg in Command of the Army of Tennessee

Situation

It was quite atypical to depose a commander whose army had just won a major battle. Yet since the Kentucky Campaign of 1862, Bragg had so dismayed his junior commanders that many of them called for his resignation. Bragg's failure to order the pursuit of Rosecrans's Army of the Cumberland had forced him to conduct a siege against Chattanooga. This action only aggravated his subordinates' animosity. Made aware of this, Confederate president Jefferson Davis traveled to the Army of Tennessee's headquarters, arriving on October 9. There, he listened to the many complaints against Bragg.[36]

Options

President Davis had two options at this time: he could either keep Bragg in command or replace him. Both options would significantly impact the future of the Army of Tennessee and, ultimately, the Confederacy.[37]

Option 1

Davis had previous knowledge of Bragg's lack of support from many officers and men, especially from some of his highest-ranking subordinate generals. If Davis kept Bragg in command, dissension would likely continue unabated in the Army of Tennessee. Yet changing commanders during the siege at Chattanooga—in the middle of a campaign—could prove foolhardy. Perhaps Davis could smooth matters over with Bragg's subordinates and ask for patriotism over personal animosity?[38]

Option 2

Replacing Bragg would likely eliminate much of the dissension within the army, especially among the senior generals. These officers' cooperation with their commander was essential to maintaining the army's ability to function and, more importantly, to fight. Yet who would the replacement be? Would he be any more successful in battle? Davis believed that only one of his available West Point officers with the rank of full general would qualify as an alternate. Two generals were available for consideration, Joseph E. Johnston and P. G. T. Beauregard, and David despised them both. It was possible that a lieutenant general might qualify.[39]

Decision

Davis made the critical decision to retain Bragg as the army commander, also allowing the general to eliminate or reassign certain of his officers. Essentially supporting the status quo, Davis stressed Bragg's authority and appealed for support for him. Bragg maintained his siege of Chattanooga.[40]

Results/Impact

Davis's choice resulted in Bragg's paying less attention to his siege and instead carrying out his vendetta against some of his detractors. The animosity toward Bragg did not recede. His lack of leadership eventually resulted in the Confederate loss of Chattanooga.[41]

Bragg felt secure and was attempting to starve the Union forces out of Chattanooga. He became inattentive to the day-to-day affairs of his own army as he went about eliminating or reassigning his senior officers. He had already relieved Lieut. Gen. Leonidas Polk and Maj. Gen. Thomas Hindman from duty for their poor performance at the Battle of Chickamauga. After receiving Davis's backing, Bragg relieved Lieut. Gen. Daniel H. Hill from command and reduced Maj. Gen. Simon B. Buckner to divisional command. He restructured most of Maj. Gen. Benjamin F. Cheatham's division of Tennesseans. Bragg distributed these brigades to his own supporters, and he reassigned other units to Cheatham. Lieut. Gen. James Longstreet, who had quickly come to despise Bragg, was sent as far away as possible to defend Lookout Mountain and the Wauhatchie Valley. Desertions climbed dramatically.[42]

As will be discussed regarding another critical decision, to relieve pressure on these areas, on October 17 Bragg ordered Maj. Gen. Carter L. Stevenson's division in the direction of Knoxville to potentially capture/ protect East Tennessee. This measure reduced the Confederate siege force (although it would be recalled prior to the battle). After Longstreet's abysmal performance in the Wauhatchie Valley, which will be addressed respecting yet another critical decision, Bragg ordered Longstreet's Corps eastward. These troops were to push Maj. Gen. Ambrose Burnside's small army out of Knoxville, further reducing his siege line. Bragg would likewise send Maj. Gen. Patrick Cleburne's and Buckner's divisions eastward on November 22. Yet as he learned of increasing Union activity on the twenty-third, Bragg quickly recalled Cleburne's men.[43]

Bragg's retention set up the Army of Tennessee for failure. As noted above, Union reinforcements from Virginia were already en route to Chattanooga. After Grant reached Chattanooga on October 23, he ordered additional reinforcements from Sherman's Army of the Tennessee to join him. This request boded ill for Confederate odds of success. Bragg's alternative was to keep what men he had and prepare for a breakout by Grant, while also concentrating on better food and supplies for his men. Better use of his cavalry (Maj. Gen. Joseph Wheeler led an abortive raid north from September 30 to October 9) would have reassured Bragg that movement to Knoxville was not necessary.[44]

Alternate Decision and Scenario

Had President Davis replaced Bragg with another officer, what might have occurred? Perhaps either Gen. Joseph E. Johnston, healed from his wounding at Seven Pines, or Lieut. Gen. William J. Hardee, the senior corps commander, might have been placed in command. Although Longstreet sought and expected this post, Davis was not impressed with his obvious attempts for promotion and independent authority. Whomever Davis might have alternatively appointed would likely have spent less time infighting and more time building up what forces he had. At least initially, the replacement commander would probably have garnered senior officers' respect and cooperation. Whether that would have been enough to contain Grant in Chattanooga remains doubtful. Grant increased his command strength in the city to a point at which it was unlikely to remain bottled up.[45]

Lincoln Decides to Consolidate the Three Western Departments

Situation

What the Union had been missing within the Western Theater was coordinated actions and movements by the three department commanders: Grant of the Department of Tennessee, Rosecrans of the Department of the Cumberland, and Maj. Gen. Ambrose Burnside of the Department of the Ohio. Maj. Gen. Henry W. Halleck, the general-in-chief, had not successfully managed the three leaders, resulting in inefficient military planning. It was natural for each commander to protect his own department and its army, believing his to be the most important. As a result, there was little incentive for the departmental commanders to work together. This situation was also prevalent among the Confederate departments and armies.[46]

With Rosecrans's defeat at Chickamauga, Lincoln realized that a command change was probably necessary for the Army of the Cumberland. He also understood that better oversight was essential for continued Union success in the Western Theater. With one general in command of the Western Theater, a more coordinated effort by the three armies in the three departments could potentially ensure eventual victory. In Maj. Gen. Ulysses S. Grant, Lincoln knew he had a general capable of successfully administering this consolidated department.[47]

Options

Lincoln had two options. He could leave the departments independent but order them to cooperate, or he could create a command structure over all three.[48]

Option 1

Lincoln may have believed that he could force the three departments to work together. However, this task would have been difficult to manage from

Major General Ulysses S. Grant, USA. Library of Congress.

Washington, DC. Slow compliance, if any, would be a likely result, and a myriad of excuses would make this a tough decision for Lincoln to enforce.[49]

<u>Option 2</u>

Lincoln could create an overall command structure for the Western Theater and place the three departments under its commander. He knew that he had Ulysses S. Grant, a successful general flush from winning his second major campaign, available to lead the combined departments.[50]

Decision

On October 16 President Abraham Lincoln made the critical decision to unite the Western Theater's three departments within the newly created Military Division of the Mississippi. That same day Grant was appointed to command this division. His leadership now allowed for a coordinated effort and a continuation of the success that various Western Theater commanders had enjoyed. Grant had a proven record of results and was a known fighter. Grant had successfully led the campaign to seize Forts Henry and Donelson, capturing some 14,000 prisoners, and also the Vicksburg Campaign, netting some 29,500 additional prisoners. As Lincoln himself phrased it, now the Mississippi River could "flow unvexed to the sea." The president considered Grant a general who would keep up the struggle, and who had been largely successful in the field.[51]

Results/Impact

This critical decision would ultimately result in Grant, now an army group commander (in modern terms), making several more critical decisions that broke the siege at Chattanooga and positioned his forces for success the following year. As will be discussed in relation to forthcoming critical decisions, Grant opened the "Cracker Line" and resupplied his command in Chattanooga. He was able to coordinate the actions of the Armies of the Tennessee and the Cumberland, as well as those of the Eleventh and Twelfth Corps under the command of Hooker, into successful attacks on Bragg's Army of Tennessee. Consequently, Chattanooga was freed and would provide an excellent starting location for the Atlanta Campaign in 1864. Grant's success at Chattanooga (his third campaign) would solidify his reputation as an effective combat general, and ultimately gain him promotion to lieutenant general and general-in-chief of the Union armies.[52]

Lincoln's consolidation of commands under Grant triggered a chain of fortuitous events, including the quick restoration of the supply line to Chattanooga (which the Confederates had severely compromised), a consolidation of forces, and ultimately the breakout of Chattanooga via the battle of that same name. It is unlikely that any other general would have made all of these events happen as fast as Grant did. Grant simply refused to let interference impinge on necessary actions. Had he not been given overall command, it is quite possible that the Union force left in Chattanooga would have been forced to abandon the city and escape into Middle Tennessee to regain a viable supply line. Doing so would have set back the Union war effort and success by many months.[53]

Alternate Decision and Scenario

Had Lincoln instead decided to let three separate departments continue operating in the Western Theater, the Battle of Chattanooga (or Missionary Ridge) would not likely have occurred. Had Maj. Gen. William S. Rosecrans, unlucky loser of the Battle of Chickamauga, been retained in command in

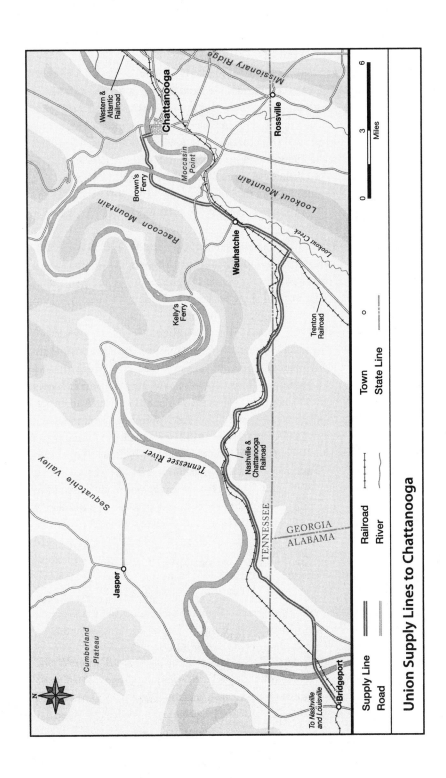

Union Supply Lines to Chattanooga

Chattanooga with his Army of the Cumberland, the prospects of Union success would have been slim. While waiting for the arrival of Hooker's twenty-three thousand men, Rosecrans's own men and animals were facing a severe reduction of supplies of all types. Yet he did little to fix that problem. Charles Dana, assistant secretary of war and, in effect, a spy for Stanton and the War Department, characterized the situation as follows: "All this precious time is lost because our dazed and mazy commander cannot perceive the catastrophe that is close upon us." Likewise, Lincoln made his famous statement that Rosecrans had been acting "confused and stunned like a duck hit on the head." In fairness, Rosecrans was working to eventually open the "Cracker Line."[54]

Lincoln's other option would have been replacing Rosecrans with Maj. Gen. George Thomas. Serving under Rosecrans, Thomas was commander of the Fourteenth Corps in the Army of the Cumberland. His defensive rear-guard action at the Battle of Chickamauga saved the Army of the Cumberland from annihilation and earned him the nickname "Rock of Chickamauga." Seemingly never in a rush, Thomas was an excellent general who never lost a battle. Certainly, he would have been a steadying influence as commander of the Army of the Cumberland, one able to attack the supply problem faced by Union forces in Chattanooga. Thomas was somewhat validated by Grant's selecting him to replace Rosecrans. This action was one of Grant's first upon his appointment to his new command. Thomas served under Grant as commander of the Army of the Cumberland during the Battle of Chattanooga, and he would continue in that capacity under Maj. Gen. William T. Sherman during the Atlanta Campaign. Had he been Rosecrans's replacement with that army remaining an independent department, Thomas likely would have fixed the supply line, refitted, added more men and animals, and ultimately conducted a similar assault to fight his way out of Chattanooga.[55]

Grant Orders the "Cracker Line" Opened

Situation

The supply line for the Union Army of the Cumberland in Chattanooga had been interdicted by the Confederate Army of Tennessee. One exception to the damage was a long, inefficient line through Jasper, Tennessee, and up to the Anderson Road that then took a tortured journey southeast into Chattanooga. Northern soldiers and animals were slowly starving. Some hungry soldiers would try and sneak off with corn supplied to feed the horses. Unsurprisingly, morale was low.[56]

The Union supply line ran south from Louisville to Nashville, then south and east into Chattanooga. Railroads extended south from Louisville through Nashville to Stephenson and Bridgeport, Alabama, then northeast into Chattanooga. Trains provided the most reliable means of supply, though steamboats plying the rivers were also an option. However, rivers could become too shallow during the summer and freeze during the winter.[57]

In addition to the railroad, the Tennessee River wound from Bridgeport, past Chattanooga, and toward Knoxville. Thus steamboats could supplement rail transport for much of the year. Roads south and north of the Tennessee River provided additional supply routes. However, once Bragg and his army surrounded much of Chattanooga, Lieut. Gen. James Longstreet's corps, which occupied Lookout Mountain and some of Lookout Valley west of Chattanooga, was able to interdict the railroad, river, and roads. The only supply line left to the Union was a very steep, winding road that bypassed Lookout Valley many miles to the north. This route was incapable of handling large numbers of wagons. It also required a significant percentage of the wagon contents to be dedicated to fodder for the animals, reducing the amount of supplies destined for Chattanooga. Additionally, ammunition, clothing, and other necessities required by Rosecrans's army were unavailable. Something had to be done, yet Rosecrans reacted slowly. When Grant arrived in Chattanooga on October 23, he was appalled by the supply situation and knew it must be rectified immediately.[58]

Options

Grant could either open a viable supply line or retreat from Chattanooga.[59]

Option 1

To open a viable supply line, Grant discovered an existing plan with which Rosecrans had grappled. Brig. Gen. William F. "Baldy" Smith had led a controversial life in the Union army. Rosecrans kept him away from direct command at Chattanooga by assigning him chief engineer of the Army of the Cumberland. Upon his arrival, Smith quickly realized the problem confronting Rosecrans. Most supply routes were interdicted by the Confederates in and near the Wauhatchie Valley or the Tennessee River. Only one lengthy, treacherous route was in service, and it could not keep up with the demand for supplies. Mules were dying all along the route from lack of feed and the road's brutal terrain. After examining the supply situation, Smith developed a plan to drastically improve it, and he presented his idea to Rosecrans on October 18. The next day he made a reconnaissance to Brown's Ferry, the key

Brigadier General William F. "Baldy" Smith,
USA. The Photographic History of the Civil
War, Vol.10, 183.

to his plan. Rosecrans took the scheme under consideration. Union troops
would need to capture this ferry to open up the supply line critical to the men
camped in and around Chattanooga. The day after Grant's arrival on October 23, Smith presented his plan to Grant.[60]

Option 2

Grant's other option was to try and move his army, most likely west through
Lookout Valley, and retreat from Chattanooga. This choice would allow him
to reattach to a viable supply line. With enough men and a light defense by
Longstreet, Grant may have been able to escape Chattanooga to fight another
day. However, he was not one to retreat: he would rather take the offensive.
This option would be distasteful to him, as it would cause the loss of Chattanooga and place Burnside in increased danger at Knoxville. Moreover, evacuating Federal troops would delay the recapture of Chattanooga, postponing
plans for a campaign farther into the Confederacy's interior.[61]

Decision

On October 24 Grant quickly ordered Baldy Smith to implement his plan
to reestablish a supply line into Chattanooga. Soldiers labeled this connec-

tion the "Cracker Line." A reliable way to deliver provisions to Chattanooga was absolutely essential for maintaining the Army of the Cumberland, which was surrounded by Confederates, and for bringing reinforcements, including animals, into the city. This route would utilize Brown's Ferry and a road out of Confederates' range. The latter would be driven from Lookout Valley in conjunction with Hooker's army advancing up Lookout Valley. Once the "Cracker Line" was established, the Army of the Cumberland could be resupplied and refitted into fighting condition. Grant would also be able to order reinforcements to Chattanooga to increase the likelihood of success for a breakout maneuver.[62]

Results/Impact

Grant placed Smith in command of the operation. Smith ordered pontoon boats built, and under the cover of night, these boats, manned by volunteers from Brig. Gen. William Hazen's brigade, loaded on the east side of Moccasin Bend, floated undetected south and then north around Moccasin Bend, and landed on the west side of Brown's Ferry. Hazen's men captured the poorly defended ferry and were quickly reinforced. Hooker's divisions at Stevenson, Alabama, were ordered to march to the Wauhatchie Valley, west of Brown's Ferry. The Rebel response was poorly planned by Longstreet. The resulting night offensive culminated in the Battle of Wauhatchie, won by Brig. Gen. John Geary and his division of the Twelfth Corps, who were left positioned in Lookout Valley. This victory opened the road and the Tennessee River, much to Bragg's dismay. Grant was then able to resupply his command, accept additional reinforcements, and plan to break the siege.[63]

Alternate Decision and Scenario

Grant's other option would have been to reluctantly abandon the city and retreat back into Middle Tennessee. While saving most of his men and some animals, this choice would have been a major setback for Union advances in the Western Theater. Additionally, it would likely have delayed the Atlanta Campaign. Fortunately for the Lincoln administration and the Union cause, Grant was not the kind of general to sit back and hope for the best.[64]

Once Grant saw that the "Cracker Line" was opened, he resupplied his army and increased the provisions capability to accommodate his reinforcements as they arrived in Chattanooga. These reinforcements would soon have a critical effect on the situation.[65]

Major General William T. Sherman, USA.
Library of Congress.

Grant Orders Sherman to Proceed Directly to Chattanooga

Situation

Grant was a confident general and felt that he could reasonably reopen a supply line to Chattanooga. It would take time to establish enough stores for his men in the city, and he felt comfortable acquiring additional support to end the siege. Grant was aware that Hooker, with the Eleventh and Twelfth Corps from the Army of the Potomac, was on the way. But he desired additional reinforcements to better his odds of breaking the siege. On September 23, only days after the Union disaster at Chickamauga, and before Grant was placed in overall command (see Critical Decision 5) and Lincoln consolidated the three Western Departments, the War Department had ordered Grant to send troops to Chattanooga to rescue Major General Rosecrans's army. Grant immediately ordered Maj. Gen. William T. Sherman to proceed there with portions of two corps of the Army of the Tennessee. After a grueling ride of some thirteen hours, Grant, now in overall command, arrived in Chattanooga on October 23. Before he went to bed that evening, he wrote Union army general-in-chief Henry Halleck to request that Sherman be placed in command of both the Department and the Army of the Tennessee.[66]

Now that Grant was in overall command of the Military Division of the Mississippi and, perhaps more importantly, was in immediate command at Chattanooga, he wasted little time in planning how to break the siege. Moreover, he continued to acquire additional manpower. Because of his trust in Sherman, Grant's initial plan called for Sherman and his men to lead the attack on Bragg's army.[67]

Options

At this time Grant had two options: he could hurry Sherman and his men to Chattanooga, or he could utilize other manpower for his breakout attack. These other forces could include Maj. Gen. Ambrose Burnside's Ninth Corps residing in Knoxville, or Hooker's two corps.[68]

Option 1

Feeling that he was losing time, and anxious to begin his breakout from Chattanooga, Grant could order Sherman to stop repairing the railroad, leave his burdensome supply wagons behind, and proceed as quickly as possible to Chattanooga. This option would speed up Grant's timetable of operations.[69]

Option 2

In addition to Hooker's command, Grant could order or request reinforcements other than Sherman to proceed to Chattanooga. A possibility was the Ninth Corps at Knoxville. These additional forces might arrive sooner than Sherman could.[70]

Decision

On October 27 Grant ordered Sherman to stop repairing the Memphis and Charleston Railroad and proceed directly to Chattanooga. The repairs had resulted in a very slow advancement toward the city. Sherman immediately complied with the order, but his men continued to encounter obstacles as they neared Chattanooga. At Grant's further direction, Sherman rode ahead of his men, reaching Chattanooga on November 14. However, Sherman's troops did not begin arriving until November 21.[71]

Results/Impact

Had Sherman continued rebuilding the railroad, his arrival at Chattanooga would have been delayed for weeks, if not longer. Not only was repairing the railroad difficult, but there was also continuous harassment from the local

Confederate cavalry. Grant wisely realized that Sherman's Army of the Tennessee needed to proceed immediately to Chattanooga to participate in plans to break the siege.[72]

Grant trusted Sherman and planned to give his army the key assignment in breaking the siege of Chattanooga—enveloping the Rebel right flank. On November 16 Grant, Sherman, and other senior officers rode to a location across the Tennessee River and opposite the north end of Missionary Ridge. They concluded that Sherman would attack there.[73]

Unfortunately, Sherman's divisions unsuccessfully attacked the north end of Missionary Ridge. Maj. Gen. Patrick Cleburne's division defended this terrain. However, Sherman's attack kept Cleburne's excellent division from being utilized elsewhere, and it also provided a distraction for Bragg and his army. Grant may have won the battle without Sherman, but Sherman's presence certainly made him more confident.[74]

Alternate Decision and Scenario

Had Grant allowed him to maintain the slow pace required to repair the Memphis and Charleston Railroad, Sherman would have either arrived much later than he did or not at all. The local Confederate cavalry continuously harassed Sherman's men as they worked to rebuild the railroad. Realistically, it was unlikely that Sherman could ever get the entire length from Memphis to even Bridgeport rebuilt. As soon as one portion was completed and his men moved farther east, Rebels would dismantle it. Grant's personality was such that he simply could not bear an interminable wait for others to arrive in Chattanooga. Eventually, he might have attacked without the advantage of Sherman's leadership and his additional men—and with unknown results.[75]

Longstreet Decides Not to Fortify Lookout Valley

Situation

Among Gen. Braxton Bragg's many concerns was Lieut. Gen. James Longstreet. A successful corps commander under Gen. Robert E. Lee in the Eastern Theater, Longstreet nonetheless desired an independent army command. Yet with Lee's many successes in the Eastern Theater, he realized such a post there was unlikely. Thus Longstreet lobbied Richmond for the chance to go west and "assist" Bragg, who had been largely unsuccessful. Lee and Jefferson Davis agreed to this suggestion. Longstreet was ordered west with two divisions and a battery of artillery, but not many horses or any supply wagons. Arriving late on the evening of September 19, 1863, the second day

Lieutenant General James Longstreet, CSA. The
Photographic History of the Civil War, Vol. 10, 245.

of the Battle of Chickamauga, Longstreet found Bragg's headquarters near midnight. To accommodate Longstreet, Bragg had reorganized his army into two wings, placing Longstreet in command of the newly designated left wing. Longstreet quickly determined that he was more capable to command than Bragg, which was why he had lobbied to go west. When Longstreet and President Davis met soon after, Davis made his support for Bragg clear. Longstreet would not, at least at that time, be considered for army command. For these reasons, relations between Longstreet and Bragg quickly soured. During the aforementioned meeting, Davis also gave Bragg the authority to replace or reassign as many of his enemies as he felt necessary. Though Bragg accomplished this feat, Longstreet was simply too politically connected and successful to be removed.[76]

Longstreet and his two divisions were assigned to defend Lookout Mountain and Lookout Valley and prevent the departure of any troops from Chattanooga. Longstreet's forces were also to thwart additional Union reinforcements' arrival from the west. This was a clear order from Bragg. However, Longstreet had devised his own theory as to the direction of the eventual Union approach, and it did not concern the Wauhatchie Valley. He believed that any Northern force moving from Bridgeport to the east would cross Sand Mountain to the west of Lookout Mountain. Federal troops would subsequently enter the valley opposite Johnson's Crook, some twenty miles south of the tip of Lookout Mountain. Marching to Johnson's Crook, the Yankees would ascend a wagon road there to the top of Lookout Mountain, then outflank Longstreet's position. This appeared to be an illogical approach for the expected Union reinforcements. Infighting within his own corps compounded Longstreet's situation. Therefore Bragg refused his request to position men on the south side of Lookout Mountain.[77]

Options

Three options were available to Longstreet. He could obey Bragg's orders to fortify both Lookout Mountain and Lookout Valley. He could ignore Bragg's orders and fortify Lookout Mountain facing to the south. Or he could comply with Bragg's orders while maintaining vigilance to the south.[78]

Option 1

His first option was to obey orders and fortify both Lookout Mountain and Lookout Valley, with emphasis on interdicting the Union supply line into Chattanooga. This option would keep a major supply line from being reestablished through Lookout Valley—a critical need for the Yankees under siege in Chattanooga. This order of Bragg's seemed logical. It required Longstreet's men to be positioned to guard the valley. The advantage of guarding Lookout Valley was that the Union supply line and reinforcements continued to be interdicted. Yet this situation did not mean that due diligence was not to be maintained elsewhere to monitor Yankee movements.[79]

Option 2

Longstreet saw that a Union approach to Chattanooga from a location across southern Lookout Mountain had not been considered. If undetected, this tactic would catch the Rebels unawares and overwhelm them. Therefore, Longstreet believed that Confederate troops needed to observe any potential Union activity south of his position. Specifically, he wanted a good portion of his men stationed where they could surveil southern Lookout Mountain and Johnson's Crook and quickly detect any surprise movements. Bragg, however, felt Union movements in this area were unlikely, and he forbade Longstreet from sending forces there. The disadvantages of this decision went beyond the fact that Union movements could catch Confederates off guard. If positioned farther south. Rebel troops would be far less capable of controlling

Lookout Valley. The valley was the more likely location for Union supply and reinforcement movements to take place.[80]

Option 3

A commonsense option to satisfy both Bragg's orders and Longstreet's concern over a Federal advance from the south was fortifying Lookout Mountain and Valley while keeping south Lookout Mountain under observation. Doing so required a plan to reinforce whichever location was the objective of the Yankee advance. The advantage of this option was that Longstreet could comply with Bragg's orders, as required by his place in the chain of command, while still ordering observers to the area of concern. The only disadvantage was the technical violation of Bragg's orders through the assignment of a very small, easily overlooked cadre of pickets to south Lookout Mountain.[81]

Decision

Longstreet ignored Bragg's orders and made the critical decision to prepare for a Union advance from the south. Several important ramifications, all of them negative, resulted from this critical decision.[82]

Results/Impact

Realistically, Longstreet failed to perform at anywhere near the level demanded of a lieutenant general. Lookout Valley was the obvious path for a supply line to be reestablished, and he should have assigned a large portion of his command to prevent that eventuality. Instead, he placed two regiments in the valley, the Fourth and the Fifteenth Alabama. The former disrupted Haley's Trace, the road on the north side of the Tennessee River, but these units were otherwise an entirely inadequate defensive force. Longstreet sent no scouts down Lookout Valley to report on any advances by Yankee reinforcements.[83]

Longstreet's assignment included protecting the Wauhatchie Valley just north of Lookout Mountain—the best route for what would become Grant's "Cracker Line." Unfortunately, in spite of his incorrect theory of a Union advance from the south, he neglected to send out scouts to verify this unlikely concept. Nor did he send scouts toward Bridgeport to ascertain any Union movement from that location. Longstreet's critical decision to inadequately defend the Wauhatchie Valley allowed Grant to easily reestablish his supply line. The troops in Chattanooga were resupplied, and additional provisions accumulated for the arrival of the corps commanded by Hooker and Sherman en route.[84]

Even though it was quite obvious that the easiest and simplest route into Chattanooga from the west was through Lookout Valley, Longstreet virtually ignored it. Only a couple of regiments were sent to defend the area. Even the capture of Brown's Ferry early on October 27 did not seem to disturb Longstreet. When Bragg learned of the capture, he was furious. Confronting Longstreet on the morning of October 28, Bragg had barely arrived atop Lookout Mountain when a messenger informed him that an enemy force was a mere six miles away. Federal soldiers were marching toward Brown's Ferry and Chattanooga. When escorted to Sunset Rock on the west side of Lookout Mountain, Longstreet and Bragg were astonished to observe, fourteen hundred feet below them and less than a mile away, the head of Maj. Gen. Joseph Hooker's two corps striding toward the small town of Wauhatchie. It was obvious to Bragg that Longstreet's procrastination in aggressively fortifying the valley had placed the Rebels in a serious predicament.[85]

Longstreet then ordered an attack, not on the entrenched Union soldiers at Brown's Ferry, but on a small force of Hooker's encamped at Wauhatchie in Lookout Valley. This command devolved into a late-night attack, which was unusual for the Civil War. The Confederate assault failed at Wauhatchie and at Smith's Hill to counter reinforcements that Hooker led from Brown's Ferry. With his supply line reestablished, Grant was able to refit his men in Chattanooga and bring in additional support, a major blow to Bragg's seige.[86]

Longstreet's performance at Lookout Mountain/Valley was not equal to what had been expected of him. While his personal aspirations had not been met, a man of his rank was nonetheless required to cooperate with his commander. In this, he was a true disappointment to the Confederacy.[87]

Alternate Decision and Scenario

Had Longstreet adequately commanded a corps in Bragg's army and carried out Bragg's orders to judiciously guard and protect Lookout Valley from enemy intrusion, the chances of the Union reestablishing its supply line may well have been seriously diminished. Grant might even have been forced to retreat from Chattanooga. Had he aggressively attacked the Union force under Brig. Gens. William Hazen and John B. Turchin at Brown's Ferry when it landed, Longstreet might have effected a severe Union setback. Likewise, an aggressive defense of Lookout Valley might have eliminated the "Cracker Line." Supplies would then have had to travel the much longer northern route, which required animals to have additional forage. Grant then might have had to retreat over the very same inefficient northern supply line.[88]

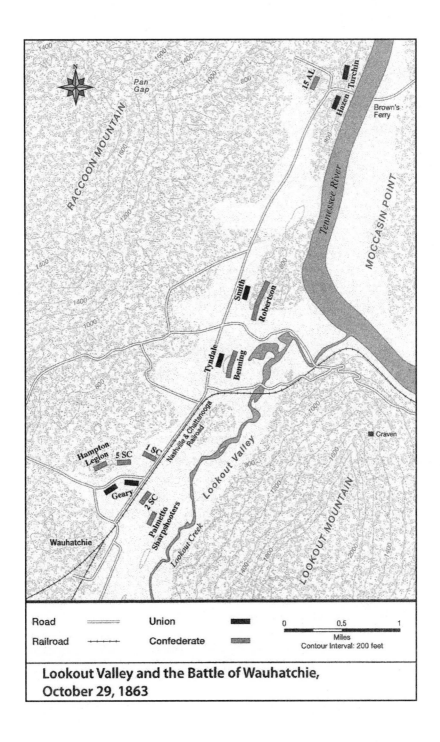

**Lookout Valley and the Battle of Wauhatchie,
October 29, 1863**

Legend:
Road
Railroad
Union
Confederate

0   0.5   1
Miles
Contour Interval: 200 feet

Had Longstreet further demonstrated his aggressiveness, he might also have confronted Hooker and his two corps upon their entrance into Lookout Valley. He could have halted the Northern advance, giving Bragg more time to evaluate the situation. Yet such was not the case. Allowing the Union to recapture Lookout Valley went a long way toward allowing the opening of the "Cracker Line," permitting Grant to resupply all of his various units.[89]

Bragg Decides that Longstreet Will Capture Knoxville

Situation

While Maj. Gen. Ulysses S. Grant was gathering additional troops to assist in his planned breakout from Chattanooga, Gen. Braxton Bragg continued to reduce his siege force. President Davis was anxious to rid Eastern Tennessee of Maj. Gen. Ambrose Burnside's Ninth Corps, now located in Knoxville. Davis did not want Burnside to come to the relief of Chattanooga. Nor did he want Grant to dispatch reinforcements to Burnside in Knoxville. As a result, Davis requested that Bragg send additional troops to Knoxville to prevent Burnside from vacating that city. This appeal played into Bragg's hands.[90]

On October 17 Bragg had dispatched Maj. Gen. Carter L. Stevenson's division east to help stop Maj. Gen. Ambrose Burnside's small army near Knoxville from advancing toward Chattanooga. On the evening of October 22, Bragg ordered Brig. Gen. John K. Jackson's division to assist Stevenson. Bragg further augmented Confederate forces there with Maj. Gen. Joseph Wheeler's cavalry corps.[91]

Bragg knew that he was stuck with Longstreet as long as Longstreet's divisions remained in his army. When pushed, Davis flatly denied Longstreet command of the Army of Tennessee. Longstreet became petulant, as seen in his actions at Lookout Mountain and Valley. Neither Bragg nor Longstreet dealt with each other unless absolutely necessary.[92]

Bragg now had the authority to rid himself of or deal with the dissident officers within his army. Due to Longstreet's excellent reputation as a corps commander and his political connections, Bragg was wise enough not to directly dismiss him. Yet he still wanted Longstreet out of his command. At the end of October, Davis advised Bragg that if he did not want Longstreet to advance toward the Union supply line at Bridgeport, he could perhaps order Longstreet to capture Knoxville. In return, Davis would have Lieut. Gen. William J. Hardee bring two brigades with him when he joined the army. Hardee had replaced Lieut. Gen. Leonidas Polk, whom Bragg had removed for malfeasance during the Battle of Chickamauga. Davis's idea gave Bragg new options.[93]

Options

Bragg had three options for dealing with Longstreet. He could keep Longstreet under much closer observation. Alternatively, he could send Longstreet and his corps to relieve Knoxville. Finally, Bragg could recommend the return of Longstreet and his divisions to Lee's Army of Northern Virginia.[94]

Option 1

Bragg had the option of placing Longstreet and his two divisions along Missionary Ridge, where he could provide direct supervision and demand cooperation. This choice would rely on the theory that Longstreet could hardly refuse direct, legitimate orders, although he had previously. By reorganizing his army, eliminating Lieut. Gens. Leonidas Polk and Daniel H. Hill, and reassigning other troublemakers, Bragg could assign a more reliable command to protect Lookout Mountain and Lookout Valley. Longstreet would not be as able to associate independently with the powerful anti-Bragg circle of generals.[95]

Option 2

Under the guise of obeying a request from President Davis, Bragg could detach Longstreet and his two divisions and order them to march to and capture Knoxville. This option would rid Bragg of the insufferable Longstreet while complying with Davis's wishes. However, it would significantly reduce Bragg's available manpower, even with the promised two additional brigades.[96]

Option 3

Bragg could recommend that Longstreet and his corps return to General Lee's Army of Northern Virginia, or anywhere else Davis desired. While this choice would deprive Bragg of Longstreet's two divisions, it would relieve Bragg from having to deal with Longstreet.[97]

Decision

On November 4 Bragg ordered Longstreet to advance to Knoxville with his two divisions, repairing the railroad as he moved east. With little logistical support, Longstreet was furious but had little recourse. Many of Bragg's command were not sorry to see Longstreet leave. Longstreet soon discovered that his seventeen thousand men were outnumbered by Burnside's twenty thousand at Knoxville, reducing the chance for a quick victory to further improve his reputation.[98]

Results/Impact

While potentially aiding Confederate operations east of Chattanooga and ridding Bragg of his now-despised rival, sending Longstreet to Knoxville reduced Bragg's Army of Tennessee by 17,000 men. Though he gained short-term relief by not having to deal with Longstreet, Bragg reduced his siege strength to a level inadequate to cover his lines around Chattanooga.[99]

On September 18, the beginning of the Battle of Chickamauga, with the inclusion of Longstreet and his corps, Bragg and his Confederates numbered about 66,000, compared to Rosecrans's 58,000 Yankees. The Confederate numbers included Longstreet and his corps. This was the first and only time Southern troops outnumbered Northern ones in the Western Theater. By October 1 Bragg's strength was down to 47,500, while the Union's was down to 35,000. Yet by November 23, just prior to the Battle Chattanooga, Bragg's army had an effective strength of only 37,000, while Grant had built up his command to 70,000. Bragg was confident in his position around Chattanooga. But he was blissfully unaware of Lincoln and Grant's actively increasing the Chattanooga area garrison. He would soon regret this dispersal of Longstreet's command.[100]

Alternate Decision and Scenario

Bragg's desire to remove Longstreet from his command might have been personally rewarding, but it placed the Army of Tennessee in a precarious position that would soon prove disastrous. With Longstreet's seventeen thousand soldiers added to Bragg's siege line, he could have kept his flanks and center more solidly fortified. Doing so might have further slowed Grant's assaults, possibly changing his victory into something less triumphant and resulting in much heavier casualties. The lack of men to maintain the siege at Chattanooga would eventually bring a Union victory. It also caused Bragg's downfall and resignation from command of the Army of Tennessee.[101]

CHAPTER 2

PRE-BATTLE, NOVEMBER 23, 1863

The day before the two-day-long Battle of Chattanooga began, three critical decisions were made that would have a significant effect on the fighting's outcome. The rise of the unexpected is typical of many battles. Commanders must recognize when their plans go awry and implement new measures to cope. These three critical decisions would come to bear on the second day of fighting, altering the entire course of the battle.

Grant Orders Sherman to Attack Bragg's Right Flank at Tunnel Hill

Situation

Maj. Gen. William T. Sherman was undoubtedly Grant's most trusted lieutenant. The two men had supported each other since the beginning of the war. As the conflict progressed, Sherman earned Grant's implicit trust to complete assignments as best he could. By this time Grant knew that he would assign Sherman and the divisions of his Army of the Tennessee the main assault on the north end of Missionary Ridge. Sherman's men would assume this responsibility as soon as they arrived in Chattanooga.[1]

After reestablishing his supply line, Grant built up and refitted his new command. He was then ready to take the offensive, a role much better suited to his military personality of action. On November 16, the day after his arrival in Chattanooga, preceding his divisions, Sherman rode with Grant,

Thomas, and Baldy Smith to a location opposite the north end of Missionary Ridge. This point was just across the Tennessee River from the north end of the ridge. After viewing the terrain, Sherman felt confident that he could assault and capture the north end of the ridge and the Rebel right flank, then advance south while rolling up the Confederate line.[2]

Grant felt that Thomas's Army of the Cumberland had not performed well at the Battle of Chickamauga. He also believed that Thomas, while an excellent general, was too slow and methodical for his own purposes. Even though Thomas was certainly more familiar with the area and situation, Grant planned to utilize his army in a supporting role. Hooker's combined force, defending Lookout Valley and the supply line, would also be utilized in a supporting role.[3]

Options

Grant was faced with four options for breaking out of Chattanooga and resuming the offensive against Bragg and his Army of Tennessee. He could attack Bragg's right flank or left flank, or both of them at once. Grant could also assault Bragg's center on Missionary Ridge.[4]

Option 1

One option was to avoid a direct frontal assault on Missionary Ridge by attacking Bragg's right flank near the ridge's northern end. After observation, Grant deduced that this area was not heavily fortified. Thomas's Army of the Cumberland was positioned in front of Missionary Ridge but did not extend to the northeast end of it. Rather than moving Thomas, it was logical to assign Sherman's army the attack on Bragg's right. If this offensive was successful, Bragg's army could be rolled up as the Union assault continued to move southwest along the ridge.[5]

Option 2

Bragg's left flank along Lookout Mountain and Valley had already been weakened by the opening of the supply line, the loss of Lookout Valley, and the departure of Longstreet. Though this area also had formidable terrain, it was not well defended by the Rebels. It provided Grant with another avenue of attack if he so desired.[6]

Option 3

Grant's third option was to combine attacks on both of Bragg's flanks with the objective of rolling up his army on Missionary Ridge on both flanks.

Grant had the manpower for this maneuver. At the same time, he could keep enough troops near Missionary Ridge to force Bragg to at least minimally man his lines at the top and bottom.[7]

Option 4

Grant's fourth option was a direct assault on Missionary Ridge. Rebel soldiers would fire at the Yankees as soon as they advanced, and they would continue to do so throughout the assault. Union artillery support would partially cover the offensive. Confederate artillery would become less lethal as the assault advanced up the ridge, as Southern gunners were unable to displace their tubes. However, some cross fire could compensate for the displacement problem. If successful, the assault would likely result in very heavy casualties. As formidable as the heights composing Missionary Ridge were, the probable outcome would be significant numbers of wounded and dead and failure to capture the ridge.[8]

Decision

Grant made the critical decision to utilize Option 3, which was to attack Bragg on both flanks. This avoided a direct assault up Missionary Ridge which appeared very unlikely to succeed. The main attack would be conducted by Sherman against Bragg's right flank while Hooker would make a diversionary attack against Bragg's left flank on Lookout Mountain.[9]

Results/Impact

When Sherman's divisions arrived in Chattanooga (without Brig. Gen. Peter Osterhaus's division, which was still at Wauhatchie), they were hidden from the Rebels' view north of the Tennessee River. This location concealed Grant's plan to attack the northern end of Missionary Ridge from Bragg. It also gave Bragg the impression that Sherman was perhaps continuing east to relieve Burnside at Knoxville. Bragg therefore ordered Cleburne's and Buckner's divisions to march to Chickamauga Station and board trains to Knoxville. Meanwhile, an elaborate plan was carried out to cross Sherman's men from the north bank of the Tennessee River to the south bank opposite north Missionary Ridge.[10]

It is important to note that on November 16, Grant, after obtaining Sherman's concurrence that a successful advance could be made toward Tunnel Hill, committed Sherman to that task. However, note that this critical decision was not carried out until the night of November 23–24. After extensive preparations on the twenty-third, Sherman's men were floated and then ferried across the Tennessee River very early on the morning of November 24. The troops were virtually undetected by Rebel pickets, whom they quickly captured. Sherman had eight brigades, and he would gain Col. Adolphus Bushbeck's brigade of Maj. Gen. Oliver O. Howard's Eleventh Corps, resulting in a total of about 16,600 soldiers. Grant ordered this command to attack and roll up the Confederate right flank, apparently established on Tunnel Hill. (The Chattanooga and Cleveland Railroad had tunneled beneath Missionary Ridge there.) Other than the few pickets Sherman's advance force easily captured, no Rebels were within two miles of Sherman's landing point. Yet Sherman, perhaps in a preview of things to come, wasted time by ordering the construction of entrenchments before moving toward Tunnel Hill. He and his divisions eventually advanced south toward Bragg's right flank. This excessive caution, which was uncharacteristic of Sherman, lost the element of surprise and benefited Bragg.[11]

Grant's plan seemed sound. He was relying on his most trusted subordinate, who was well supplied with soldiers, to attack an apparently weak point of the Confederate line. Grant also ordered an attack on Lookout Mountain, although he felt that it was not the key to escaping the confinement of the Chattanooga area. Rather, this offensive was more of a diversionary movement. Hooker was pleased with these plans; they gave him a chance at redemption for his poor performance at the Battle of Chancellorsville. There is little reason to debate Grant's decision to send Sherman to north Missionary Ridge. Sherman appeared to share Grant's need for aggressive movements, which Grant had not seen in his other corps or army commanders. Inadvertently, Bragg's line around the Union command in Chattanooga was vulnerable at his left and right flanks—at Lookout Mountain and on Missionary Ridge.[12]

This was Grant's key critical decision to enable the escape from Chattanooga once he was placed in overall command and was in the city. With his various subordinates positioned where he wanted them, this appeared to be a solid, capable scheme. However, it did not yield the results Grant had anticipated. Additional critical decisions were made as a result, and they would determine the battle's ultimate course.[13]

Alternate Decision and Scenario

Amazingly, the option to assault Missionary Ridge was the one that succeeded when Sherman's assault on Bragg's right flank at Tunnel Hill failed. This alternate critical decision to launch an offensive up Missionary Ridge was not made by Grant, but by a number of commanders of all ranks. This critical decision will be the last one on the final day of fighting that is discussed below.[14]

Grant Orders Thomas to Conduct a Reconnaissance in Force

Situation

On November 22 Union pickets observed movement from the Confederate line atop Missionary Ridge.[10] This activity was the withdrawal of Cleburne's and Buckner's divisions, which Bragg had ordered east to Knoxville. Bragg feared that Sherman's divisions were also marching in that direction, as they had been concealed from view. Grant, too, was led to believe this withdrawal could be underway. He had received a note from Bragg himself suggesting that he remove all noncombatants from Chattanooga. Was this a ruse to cover a Rebel retreat by suggesting a Rebel attack was imminent? Grant's concern was determining what exactly the Rebels were doing. He was unaware that Cleburne's and Buckner's divisions were not leading a retreat, but were on their way to assist in the capture of Knoxville.[15]

Options

Concerned about Bragg's possible retreat, Grant had two options. First, he could send a small cavalry force around Missionary Ridge to ascertain if Rebel troops were marching or boarding trains toward Knoxville or possibly south toward Ringgold. Additionally, Grant could send a reconnaissance in force toward the Confederate picket line and Missionary Ridge positions to evaluate their response.[16]

Option 1

Sending some of Grant's limited cavalry east and south of Missionary Ridge on a reconnaissance might provide intelligence of Rebel movements and retreats. However, the scouting could be screened by Confederate cavalry, and it would require some time to complete.[17]

Option 2

A reconnaissance in force by a portion of Thomas's Army of the Cumberland might immobilize the Confederates as they observed Grant's movements and tried to decipher his intentions. This option might well forestall any retreating by the Rebels if, in fact, that was their intent. Moreover, this measure would likely result in few Union casualties.[18]

Major General George H. Thomas, USA.
The Photographic History of the Civil War,
Vol. 10, 171.

Decision

To determine whether Bragg had ordered a retreat, Grant made the critical decision to send a reconnaissance in force toward Missionary Ridge. He ordered Thomas's Army of the Cumberland to advance from the trenches surrounding Chattanooga and push the Rebel pickets back to their line at the base of Missionary Ridge. Thomas and his men complied. Brig. Gen. Thomas J. Wood, whose division was opposite a small eminence called Orchard Knob, was assigned to lead this reconnaissance in force toward it. Thomas wished to avoid any chance of failure. Thus he required the full support of his other two divisions, as well as that of Maj. Gen. O. O. Howard's two divisions. Some twenty-five thousand men were ready to advance. The order was for the reconnaissance to be conducted, and for the troops involved to then fall back into their original lines.[19]

Results/Impact

Wood's eight-thousand-man division formed. Thomas ordered Howard's Eleventh Corps to support Wood on his left and Brig. Gen. Philip Sheridan's division to support Wood on his right. Rebel leaders, not to mention Rebel pickets, were naturally astonished to observe the enemy's grand twenty-five-thousand-man display prior to venturing forth.[20]

Orchard Knob, Tennessee. Orchard Knob; George W. Skinner, *Pennsylvania at Chickamauga and Chattanooga* (William Stanley Ray Printer, 1901), 35.

The reconnaissance was successful. The Confederate pickets were quickly overrun, and many were captured before they could fall back to their entrenchments at the base of Missionary Ridge. Pleased with this movement, Grant countered his order for Thomas's men to retire back to their original lines. They would maintain this new, advanced position. Grant and other Union officers quickly observed that the Rebels were not retreating from their Missionary Ridge line. In fact, Federals could observe renewed efforts by those Confederates on the ridge.[21]

An unanticipated result of this critical decision was that Thomas's Union line had now advanced eight hundred yards toward the Rebel entrenchments at the bottom of Missionary Ridge. This position would prove immensely valuable to Grant and his men on the twenty-fifth; as it would require less ground to be covered under fire during that assault.[22]

While Grant was now satisfied that the Confederates were not evacuating Chattanooga, this Union movement resulted in Bragg's immediately ordering two actions. Incredibly, Bragg had not bothered actually fortify his line along the top of Missionary Ridge, assuming it was impregnable. He belatedly established defensive forces along the top of the ridge. The Rebels had been so confident in the natural strength of the terrain that they had not previously dug a line there. Unfortunately for the Confederates, the line to be

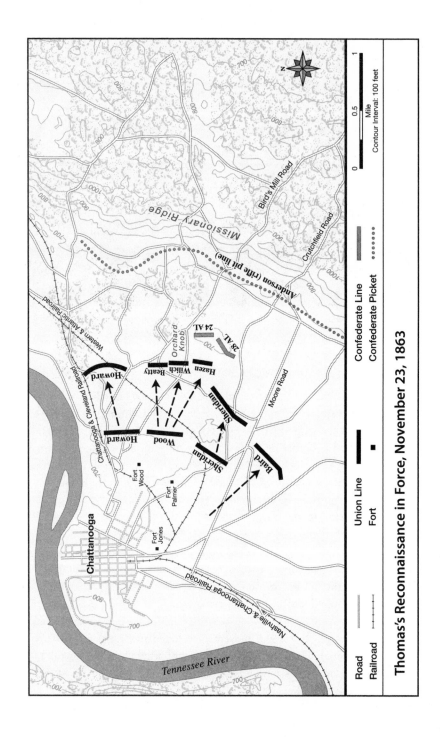

Thomas's Reconnaissance in Force, November 23, 1863

dug was on the topographical crest of the ridge, not the military crest. This circumstance will be discussed in relation to the next critical decision.[23]

The other action taken by Bragg actually went against Grant's plans for escaping from Chattanooga. Bragg began to believe that Grant's forthcoming attack would be against Missionary Ridge, not Lookout Mountain. Bragg then frantically recalled Maj. Gen. Patrick Cleburne's division, which was preparing to board trains headed east to Knoxville. Cleburne moved his men and those of Brig. Gen. Alexander. W. Reynolds's brigade of Maj. Gen. Simon Buckner's division back behind Bragg's headquarters on Missionary Ridge. Cleburne's presence would shortly become a huge complication for Grant and Sherman.[24]

Alternate Decisions and Scenarios

Had Grant decided not to order this reconnaissance in force, Thomas's men would have had to advance over additional ground on the twenty-fifth. That day, Grant ordered a demonstration to the base of Missionary Ridge to distract Bragg. In covering more ground, Thomas's men would have withstood more enemy fire. Potentially many more casualties would have resulted, perhaps limiting or even canceling the subsequent assault up the ridge. Unaware of the exact actions of Bragg's Rebels, Grant may even have changed his plans or held off Sherman's initial advance.[25]

Breckinridge Orders Captain Green to Lay Out a Topographical Crest Line of Defense

Situation

Braxton Bragg was aghast upon observing Thomas's demonstration carrying Orchard Knob and the terrain on each side of it. Bragg quickly decided to meet with his corps commanders to discuss resisting a further Union advance or ordering a retreat. Maj. Gen. John Breckinridge strongly believed that if the Confederate Army of Tennessee could not hold the Missionary Ridge line, it could not hold anywhere else. Bragg decided that his army would remain on the ridge. Temporarily commanding the Missionary Ridge line in Hardee's absence, Breckinridge ordered Hardee's chief engineering officer, Capt. John W. Green, to establish a defensive line along Missionary Ridge. Only a haphazard Confederate line had wound its way along the top of the ridge for the last sixty-two days! Missionary Ridge appeared so insurmountable that Bragg and his senior commanders had given little thought to defense against an actual Federal assault.[26]

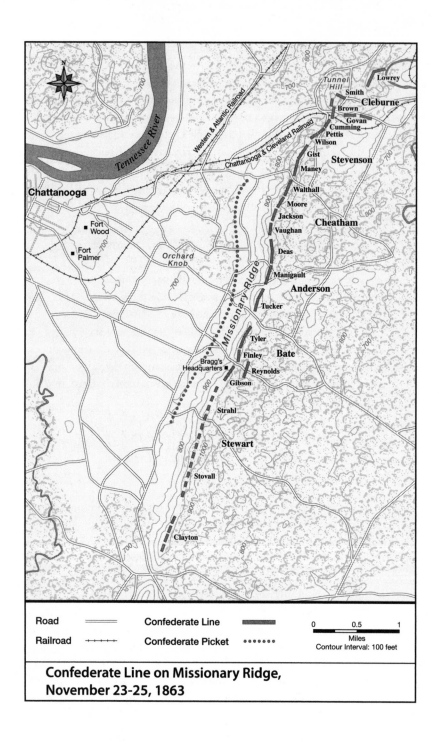

**Confederate Line on Missionary Ridge,
November 23-25, 1863**

Road

Railroad

Confederate Line

Confederate Picket

0   0.5   1
Miles
Contour Interval: 100 feet

Tennessee River

Chattanooga

Fort Wood

Fort Palmer

Orchard Knob

Western & Atlantic Railroad

Chattanooga & Cleveland Railroad

Missionary Ridge

Tunnel Hill

Lowrey

Smith

Brown

Cleburne

Govan

Cumming

Pettis

Wilson

Gist

Stevenson

Maney

Walthall

Moore

Jackson

Cheatham

Vaughan

Deas

Manigault

Anderson

Tucker

Tyler

Finley

Bate

Reynolds

Gibson

Bragg's Headquarters

Strahl

Stewart

Stovall

Clayton

Options

There were only two reasonable options for placements for a defensive line atop Missionary Ridge: the topographical crest (highest point) or the military crest.[27]

Option 1

A ridge's topographical crest runs along its highest points. While this may seem the logical location for a defensive line, fortifications and men there can be outlined against the sky and become easy targets. However, it is also easy to overshoot targets along a topographical crest. This position's other disadvantages are that it usually does not provide the best view of an assaulting force, and it often does not provide the best fields of fire.[28]

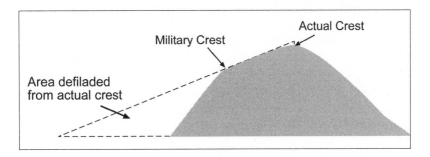

Option 2

The military crest is defined as "a fixed line on the forward slope of a hill or ridge from which maximum observation covering the slope down to the base of the hill or ridge can be obtained." It is further defined as "an area on the forward or reverse slope of a hill or ridge just below the topographical crest from which maximum observation and direct fire covering the slope down to the base of the hill or ridge can be obtained." If the main defensive position is located on the military crest, it not only gives the defensive force the maximum ability to observe the attacking force, but also allows the maximum firepower to bear upon the attacking force at the earliest opportunity.[29]

Decision

Maj. Gen. John Breckinridge made the critical decision to lay out the Confederate line on the topographical crest.[30]

Results/Impact

It is unknown exactly what instructions Captain Green received. Breckinridge, a corps commander and major general who commanded much of the Missionary Ridge position, failed to submit an after-action report. Prior to the war, Green trained as a civil engineer and spent twenty years working as one in the lumber industry. He briefly joined the Fourth Louisiana Battalion, then left to serve as senior engineer for the Vicksburg, Shreveport, and Texas Railroad. In July 1862 he was appointed a first lieutenant in the engineer corps. Green's age and experience placed him above many of his peers. He was appointed chief engineer of Hardee's corps, with the rank of captain. Competent at his job, Green finished the war as a major in the engineer corps.[31]

Due to his military and engineering experience, Green would have known the difference between the locations, and he likely would have preferred the military crest. But in the absence of Hardee, Green was apparently acting on direct orders from Breckinridge. He would have had no leeway to change them. Breckinridge's alleged drunkenness during much of the battle might have resulted in his disorientation and issuance of the faulty order to establish a topographical line. Brig. Gen. Arthur M. Manigault shed some light on the matter. Manigault, commanding a brigade in Maj. Gen. Thomas Hindman's division (temporarily commanded by Brig. Gen. Patton Anderson) observed Green moving through his brigade's position and laying out the line. Manigault was displeased with the arrangement. He told Green that he himself would fortify an appropriate line for his brigade. In response, Green reiterated that his orders were to lay out the line along the topographical crest. Unlike the rest of the Rebel line, Manigault positioned his men on the military crest, not the topographical one.[32]

Breckinridge's critical decision to position the Confederate line on the topographical crest instead of the military crest cost the Rebels the battle. As discussion of Critical Decision 18 will address, the Union attackers gained a measure of protection from Green's choice of defensive position. Rebels manning the top of the ridge remained vulnerable, yet the advancing Federal soldiers had some cover as they neared the ridge's summit. The military crest was far and away the better location for both infantry and artillery. Missionary Ridge's peak was some six hundred feet above Chattanooga, and the slope leading to it was approximately forty-five degrees—very steep. Though some cross fire capability remained, the Rebels' fields of fire were severely limited, particularly for their artillery. Many positions below the topographical crest were protected from Confederate fire. Union commands could regroup in these locations. Yankees advancing on the summit could quickly overrun the Confederate line because of the restricted fields of fire.[33]

Thomas's assault on November 25 did not stop at the bottom of the ridge as ordered, but continued successfully to the top. Rebels stationed at the peak were quickly overwhelmed. This key maneuver resulted in a significant Union victory and a rout for the Confederacy, including the loss of Chattanooga.[34] The Army of Tennessee consistently utilized the geographical crest. In the ensuing Atlanta Campaign, almost all of their works from Dalton to Kennesaw Mountain were on the geographical crest, even the defenses at Cheatham Hill. The reason for this consistent choice is so far unexplained.[35]

Alternate Decision and Scenario

Had the Rebel line been placed along the military crest, it would employed a much stronger defensive fire. At the same time, Yankee soldiers would have accessed significantly fewer protected positions in which to stop, rest, and reform before rushing the Confederate line. Rebel artillery firing canister and double canister could have decimated the Union troops assaulting the ridge. Combined with the poorly located lines at the bottom of Missionary Ridge, the defensive position on the topographical crest portended the Confederate disaster. For the Union high command, attacking a strong Rebel line after ascending such a tall, steep slope would have given Grant and his subordinates reason *not* to send Thomas's men past the Confederate trenches at the base of the ridge. It would have been virtually inconceivable for a solid line on the military crest not to resist a frontal assault and inflict heavy casualties. With Sherman stymied on the Confederate right flank, Bragg could then have more properly defended his left flank.[36]

CHAPTER 3

DAY ONE, NOVEMBER 24, 1863

The first day's fighting began with Sherman's successful crossing of the Tennessee River and an advance along northern Missionary Ridge. Meanwhile, Hooker's three divisions fought on Lookout Mountain. Though Hooker achieved success, Sherman did not, forcing Grant to change his plan of battle. Three critical decisions made on this day would shape the outcome of the following day's engagements.

Bragg Decides That Cleburne Will Protect the Right Flank at Tunnel Hill

Situation

Bragg was up early on November 24. His immediate concern was preparation for possible attacks on his line at the base and the top of Missionary Ridge. As previously noted, Bragg had had no inkling that Grant might attack Missionary Ridge until Grant's reconnaissance in force the day before. Bragg's assumption now was that Thomas's command might be his most immediate threat. Thus it was another shock to Bragg when his morning reconnaissance revealed Sherman and his divisions moving toward Tunnel Hill. The previous evening Bragg had ordered Cleburne to send Brig. Gen. Lucius Polk's brigade to guard the Confederate right flank near Tunnel Hill, toward the northern end of Missionary Ridge. Brig. Gen. Marcus Wright's brigade arrived at Chickamauga Station that morning. Bragg sent the unit to the mouth of South Chickamauga Creek to protect supplies at Chickamauga Station and cover a possible line of retreat. Bragg now had two brigades to protect his army from Sherman's advance with four divisions.[1]

Options

Bragg had three options for shielding his right flank from being overrun. He could shift some part of his army to meet the looming assault on his right flank. He could also reposition his right flank farther southwest and reinforce it there. Finally, he could retreat to a more defensible location.[2]

Option 1

Bragg had finally recognized that his right flank was not only vulnerable but about to be overrun. If he quickly sent reinforcements to these troops, he might be able to stop Sherman. Bragg could order his best division commander, Maj. Gen. Patrick Cleburne, to bring the rest of his division to Tunnel Hill and defend the right flank there.[3]

Option 2

Another option for Bragg was to recall troops already stationed at Tunnel Hill and establish a strong defensive line closer to the center of his army. Though much less desirable to defend than Tunnel Hill, this location might allow more time to prepare a proper defense. It would also reduce the length of Bragg's line on Missionary Ridge and allow more troops to defend his right flank.[4]

Option 3

Bragg's third option was to cede the Missionary Ridge position and retreat to another defensible location farther south. Moving south would give the Union undisputed control of Chattanooga and the railroads, except for the Western and Atlantic Railroad. This measure would allow Bragg to conduct an orderly retreat. Suitable defensive positions existed at Ringgold and Dalton. However, Breckinridge was reputed to have stated that "if they couldn't fight here with such advantage of position, they couldn't fight anywhere"[5]

Decision

Around 2:00 p.m. Bragg ordered Cleburne and his three remaining brigades to march rapidly to Tunnel Hill, entrench, and defend the Confederate right flank under immediate threat from Sherman. Cleburne hastened in advance

Major General Patrick R. Cleburne, CSA.
Library of Congress.

of his brigades and evaluated the situation facing the exposed right flank. He realized that he did not have enough men to protect the right flank and tie in with the Confederate line farther south on Missionary Ridge. He requested reinforcements, and more troops were dispatched. Meanwhile, Cleburne placed his men as they arrived, just ahead of the initial Union assault.[6]

Results/Impact

Initially, Bragg simply reacted to Grant's critical decision ordering Sherman's assault on Missionary Ridge and recalling the two divisions that had been sent to capture Knoxville. Bragg subsequently made his own critical decision—using his best division commander to shore up and defend his exposed right flank. This timely choice staved off defeat.[7]

One of Cleburne's brigades, commanded by Brig. Gen. James A. Smith, was placed at Tunnel Hill, and skirmishers were ordered out to observe Sherman's movements. These soldiers repulsed an initial Union attack by Sherman. As more of Cleburne's men continued to arrive, he placed them in the best locations for a strong defense. Lieutenant General Hardee, now on scene, assisted in placing these reinforcements. From the Rebel viewpoint, the arrival of Cleburne and his men temporarily saved the day; his brigades were some of the few units not forced to retreat on November 25.[8]

Alternate Decisions and Scenarios

Had Bragg not quickly dispatched Cleburne and his men to Tunnel Hill, his right flank might have been immediately overrun and his position atop Missionary Ridge rolled up. This was Grant's plan all along. Not sending Cleburne or any other force would have set up the Army of Tennessee for disaster. Cleburne was widely recognized as the best division commander in this Confederate army. Had Bragg assigned another commander this task, the outcome might not have been as successful. Although Bragg's choice could not save his army from eventual disaster at Chattanooga, it prevented defeat on the first day of fighting.[9]

Had Bragg reinforced his right flank where it was presently located southwest of Tunnel Hill, his reinforcements would have marched a shorter distance and arrived sooner. However, without the defensive terrain available to the Rebels at Tunnel Hill, Sherman could have quickly advanced south past Tunnel Hill. He then could have sent all four divisions under his command against Bragg's right flank. In spite of Breckinridge's boast that if the Confederate army could not hold Missionary Ridge, it could not hold any other location, and given the disparate numbers on each side, Bragg might have been wise to order a retreat at this time. A retreat might have been conducted in an orderly fashion instead of devolving into the rout that eventually took place. It might also have spared the capture of so many men, cannon, and other military equipage.[10]

Sherman Decides to Entrench, and Not Attack Tunnel Hill

Situation

The usually aggressive Maj. Gen. William T. Sherman showed uncharacteristic caution during this entire movement. Concerned with the initial crossing of the Tennessee River, he should have quickly realized that no Confederates besides a few unobservant pickets were nearby. Sherman's 16,600 men were equal to about one-third of the entire Confederate army present in the Chattanooga area. While his force was concentrated, the Confederate army was strung out over many miles along Missionary Ridge, across Chattanooga Valley, and on Lookout Mountain. It was highly unlikely that a significant Confederate force would advance on Sherman. Yet Sherman was so wary of an attack that he had his men entrench south of the Tennessee River before advancing on Tunnel Hill. This caution cost him not only the element of surprise, but also precious hours of daylight in short supply in late November. With all of his men across the river, Sherman finally began his advance toward Tunnel Hill at 1:30 p.m. in a cold drizzle. He had approximately four hours of daylight to capture his objective some two miles away.[11]

Mistakenly assuming that Missionary Ridge was one continuous elevation, Sherman initially arrived at Billy Goat Hill, not Tunnel Hill. Tunnel Hill was a mile away and separated by a significant valley. Union forces had only an hour of daylight left to advance to Tunnel Hill. Sunset was at 5:31 p.m., with full dark at 5:59 p.m. A full moon would rise at 5:09 p.m., but the daylong rain and mist would have obscured any moonlight.[12]

Options

At this point Sherman had three options: He could order an all-out assault against Tunnel Hill with every available unit. He could also direct his brigades to advance and entrench on the northern end of Tunnel Hill. Finally, Sherman could entrench on Billy Goat Hill to protect his brigades from a possible (although highly unlikely) Rebel counterattack.[13]

Option 1

Sherman could continue moving southwest along Missionary Ridge, descending down Billy Goat Hill, crossing the intermediate valley, and assaulting up Tunnel Hill with all of his brigades. This option was in keeping with Grant's orders and would be key to winning the battle. Tunnel Hill was already fortified by some of Cleburne's men, and its constricted terrain would certainly hinder an assault there. Yet Sherman had a sizable advantage in manpower over Cleburne's one brigade, even though the latter continued to receive reinforcements.[14]

Option 2

Sherman could order a brigade or two to make a reconnaissance of the Confederate defenses on Tunnel Hill, then have those troops entrench nearby. This measure would likely hold the Rebels in position and keep them from assaulting Sherman. Moreover, ascertaining the Rebel strength would allow him to better prepare an attack on Tunnel Hill.[15]

Option 3

With darkness quickly approaching, Sherman could remain atop Billy Goat Hill and entrench. This option would give him maximum protection in the event of a Rebel attack, and he could resume the movement to Tunnel Hill

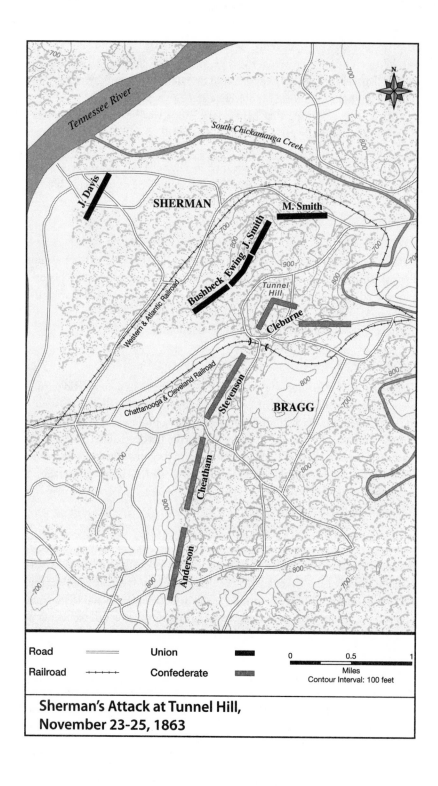

**Sherman's Attack at Tunnel Hill,
November 23-25, 1863**

early the next morning. However, this choice would also provide the Confederate command with time to reinforce their position at Tunnel Hill. The enemy could then potentially forestall the Union advance, which was clearly not what Grant expected.[16]

Decision

Sherman made the critical decision to entrench his men in defiance of Grant's orders. Other than sending a few troops to contest possession of Tunnel Hill, Sherman did little to carry out his assigned task. Daylight was quickly fading, and he believed he could not advance.[17]

Results/Impact

Grant, of course, was fully expecting Sherman to quickly capture the north end of Missionary Ridge and begin to roll up the right flank of the entrenched Confederate army. Confident in Sherman's ability, Grant awaited his confirmation of the advance's successful completion. However, Sherman had called off the advance toward the Confederate position on the ridge above Tunnel Hill. Normally more aggressive, Sherman had erred on the side of caution. This deviation from Grant's orders and plan of attack would significantly alter the battle's future course, forcing Grant to revise his plan.[18]

Alternate Decisions and Scenarios

Once his brigades were across the Tennessee River, Sherman's most obvious option was quickly putting these soldiers in motion, taking advantage of the remaining daylight and the fact that a sole Rebel brigade stood between them and the northern end of Missionary Ridge. Had Sherman availed himself of this opportunity, he might have advanced the extra distance to the Confederate position on the real northern end of the ridge at Tunnel Hill.[19]

Instead of chafing over his misidentifying the northern end of the ridge and ordering his men to stop advancing farther to the south, Sherman could have continued his advance. His men would have covered rough terrain. But their overwhelming numbers meant they might have easily overrun the small Confederate force holding this end of the rebel line. Sherman's failure to take this action drastically altered Grant's plans. Deploying scouts and skirmishers upon crossing the river would have quickly determined that no other Confederates would oppose an advance to the top of Missionary Ridge. Sherman failed to utilize the remaining daylight by sending his troops ahead. By misusing the available daylight, disregarding the lack of enemy opposition, and ignoring Grant's desire to advance, despite his misunderstanding of the enemy's location, Sherman undermined Grant's entire plan of action. As a result, Bragg had the opportunity to effectively preserve his right flank and then aggressively defend it.[20]

Bragg Decides to Abandon Lookout Mountain

Situation

As Bragg began to grasp the significance of the Union movements, he realized that he needed to quickly shore up his defenses and prepare for an impending attack. He already knew that his defenses on Lookout Mountain were wholly inadequate, that the mountain was of little value to his defenses, and that he needed his men on the mountain to reinforce his weakened line surrounding Chattanooga.[21]

Maj. Gen. Joseph Hooker was in command of Grant's right flank in Lookout Valley. He had three divisions: Brig. Gen. Charles Cruft's of the Fourth Corps, Thomas's Army of the Cumberland; Brig. Gen. John Geary's of the Twelfth Corps, Hooker's own Army of the Potomac; and Brig. Gen. Peter Osterhaus's of the Fifteenth Corps, Sherman's Army of the Tennessee, which had not been able to cross the Tennessee River due to the pontoon bridge's failure. In conjunction with Sherman's assault on north Missionary

Lookout Mountain, Tennessee. Henry Van Ness Boynton, *Dedication of the Chickamauga and Chattanooga National Military Park, September 18–20, 1895: Report of the Joint Committee to Represent Congress at the Dedication of the Chickamauga and Chattanooga National Military Park* (Washington, DC: Government Printing Office, 1896), 5.

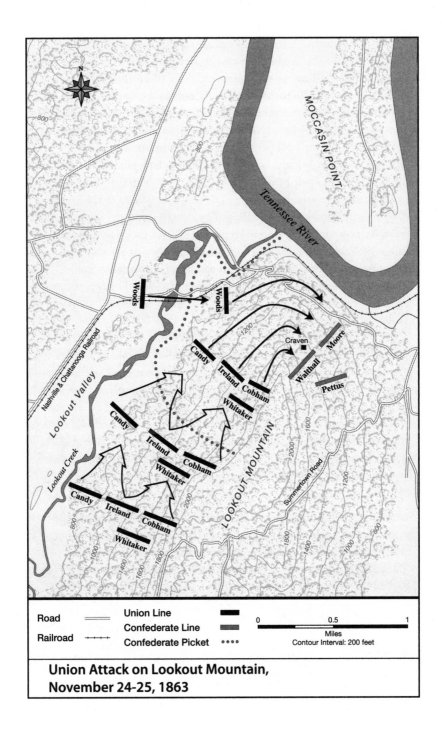

**Union Attack on Lookout Mountain,
November 24-25, 1863**

Road · · · · · · · · · ·   Union Line ▬▬▬   0   0.5   1

Railroad ┼┼┼┼┼   Confederate Line ▬▬▬   Miles

Confederate Picket ● ● ● ●   Contour Interval: 200 feet

Ridge, Grant ordered Hooker to cautiously attack Lookout Mountain if feasible. Hooker saw this command as an opportunity to regain his reputation after his colossal failure at the Battle of Chancellorsville. He successfully launched an assault along the middle of Lookout Mountain, not planning to capture the top, but to cut off the Rebels there from their fellow soldiers in the Chattanooga Valley. Hooker ultimately forced the Confederates to retreat past the Craven's House, located partway up the mountain.[22]

By this time Bragg had concluded that Grant planned to roll up the Rebel right flank, now defended by elements of Maj. Gen. Patrick Cleburne's division. Realizing the seriousness of the situation, Bragg knew that he needed to quickly reinforce the Missionary Ridge line. The troops deployed on Lookout Mountain, now under the overall command of Maj. Gen Carter Stevenson, were the only additional manpower available. Bragg was somewhat aware of the less-than-satisfactory performance of several Confederate commanders on Lookout Mountain, such as Brig. Gen. John Jackson. Further, Bragg now accepted that the Confederate position on the mountain provided little tactical value to him at this critical time.[23]

The situation at Chattanooga suddenly overcame Bragg; he was being assaulted by Grant on both flanks and potentially all points along his line. He needed to shore up his ill-prepared defenses to prepare for any additional assaults by Grant. Thus he had to weigh his options carefully.[24]

Craven's House Viewed from Union Approach. George W. Skinner, *Pennsylvania at Chickamauga and Chattanooga* (William Stanley Ray Printer, 1901), 98.

Options

At this time Bragg had three options: stand by and await additional assaults, reacting to these by shifting troops; shift brigades from his center along Missionary Ridge to strengthen his left and right flanks; or abandon his left flank on Lookout Mountain and shore up his threatened line along Missionary Ridge, further protecting his right flank and a newly established left flank.[25]

Option 1

Awaiting Grant's assault on one or more sectors of Bragg's line would allow Bragg to accurately respond to those locations under siege. But this plan of action would require time to move troops to shore up threatened defenses. Depending on who was attacked and where, Bragg's response time could simply be inadequate, allowing for a breakthrough at one or more points along his line or on his flanks. This option placed Bragg at the mercy of whatever assault(s) Grant launched, giving Grant the tactical initiative.[26]

Option 2

Bragg could shift some brigades from his center along Missionary Ridge to reinforce both his left and right flanks. Unfortunately, this measure would further weaken his center line, which appeared vulnerable for the first time because of Thomas's previous reconnaissance in force toward Bragg's center. Bragg did not have enough soldiers to adequately cover his entire line.[27]

Option 3

Bragg could reposition his left flank by abandoning Lookout Mountain. The soldiers who had occupied the mountain could help establish a new, stronger left flank and reinforce Bragg's center and right flank. His army would then be defending a shorter line, now staffed with additional manpower. However, the Rebel army was still vulnerable to attack on Bragg's weak left flank near Rossville, as well as his on right flank at Tunnel Hill. Even the possibility of an assault directly on Missionary Ridge remained.[28]

Decision

Furious at his troops' lack of effort on Lookout Mountain, at around 2:30 p.m. Bragg made the critical decision to abandon the area. Maj. Gen. Carter Stevenson, in command of the Lookout Mountain segment of the Confederate line, received orders to withdraw all Confederate troops and rejoin Bragg's army along Missionary Ridge.[29]

Results/Impact

How critical was this decision? Had Bragg left the Rebel units on Lookout Mountain, at least part of them would likely have become casualties. The three divisions under Maj. Gen. Joseph Hooker were already demonstrating their dominance on the battlefield, and the remaining Rebels on the mountain would in all likelihood have become their victims. More importantly, Bragg had finally realized the weakness of his Missionary Ridge line in comparison to Grant's heavily reinforced armies.[30]

If Bragg had not abandoned the area, he could not have reinforced his center and right. Realistically, it was already too little too late for him and his men to have any real chance for success. While absent from it, Bragg had realized that holding Lookout Mountain was not a valuable position. He was in the process of losing it anyway.[31]

Maj. Gen. Benjamin F. Cheatham had returned from leave after attempting to resign after the Battle of Chickamauga. He was on Lookout Mountain by evening, and he followed Bragg's orders to have the remaining Rebel units vacate their position. Cheatham subsequently returned command to Stevenson, who continued the retreat down into the valley.[32] The soldiers' withdrawal continued all night in rain and fog. In the morning, elements of Hooker's command placed Union flags atop Lookout Mountain, culminating the "Battle above the Clouds."[33]

Alternate Decisions and Scenarios

Awaiting Grant's next movement was not a good option. Bragg might take too long getting the right number of troops to the right place to effectively repulse a Yankee attack. Reinforcing his left flank on Lookout Mountain would only have rendered the situation along Missionary Ridge more untenable. It was obvious to Bragg that Grant had ordered an assault on his right flank now established at Tunnel Hill and would require additional reinforcements. Also, an assault on Missionary Ridge, previously discounted, now appeared to be a distinct possibility.[34]

By ordering his troops off the mountain, Bragg at least had their use for another day. The dispersal of Longstreet's divisions to Knoxville would now haunt Bragg. These troops would have been of immense value—and indeed necessary—for sustaining the Confederate grip around Chattanooga.[35]

CHAPTER 4

DAY TWO, NOVEMBER 25, 1863

The critical decisions made on the Battle of Chattanooga's first day would have a strong impact on the second and final day of the fighting. The final day's fighting and the favorable outcome for Grant and the Union were due to three critical decisions made on November 25, 1863. Sherman's failure to successfully assault Tunnel Hill gave Bragg his only success that day. Grant ordered Thomas to conduct a demonstration and capture the Confederate rifle pits and entrenchments at the bottom of Missionary Ridge. In so doing, Grant took advantage of Thomas's movement on the twenty-third, which had placed him much closer to those entrenchments. At all levels, Thomas's commanders independently resolved to disregard orders and assault Missionary Ridge. This critical decision makes the Battle of Chattanooga interesting and unique as compared to other Civil War engagements. Due to changing circumstances as the fighting evolves, battlefield commanders sometimes make critical decisions spontaneously. This was one of those times.

Sherman Decides to Attack with Two of Nine Brigades

Situation

Sherman was up early on the twenty-fifth. Having received a message from Grant around midnight, Sherman knew that he was expected to begin rolling up the Confederate right flank, which was now well fortified above Tunnel Hill, at daylight. Yet Sherman here again displayed a very uncharacteristic reluctance to advance. This hesitancy would become detrimental to the Union advance and effectively ruin Grant's plan of attack.[1]

Sherman's nine brigades had spent the night working on entrenchments that had no value if the Yankees were to advance toward the enemy on Tunnel Hill. The freezing temperatures would not have allowed most of these Federals much sleep.[2]

Options

As Sherman prepared to once again advance toward Tunnel Hill and the Confederate right flank, he had three options: attacking with a portion of his command, attacking with his entire command, or attempting to outflank the Rebel right flank at Tunnel Hill.[3]

Option 1

Sherman had some 16,600 soldiers from parts of four divisions under his command. The terrain surrounding Tunnel Hill limited the number of brigades that could attack simultaneously. He could commit enough soldiers to attack, backed by reinforcements, and hope to overrun the entrenched Rebels.[4]

Option 2

Another option for Sherman was to assign a sufficient force to surround the Rebel position at Tunnel Hill. He could conduct a double envelopment with attacks southwest of Cleburne's position along the northwest side of the ridge. Simultaneously, Sherman could maneuver brigades around to the east and then south of Tunnel Hill to outflank the defenders.[5]

Option 3

His third option was to avoid the Tunnel Hill position and breach the Rebel line at a location southeast of and behind Tunnel Hill, cutting off the Rebel right flank. This choice would cover more terrain, allowing all of Sherman's brigades to move at once and overwhelm the Rebels.[6]

Decision

As it happened, Sherman's critical decision fell in favor of Option 1. He ordered division commander Brig. Gen Hugh Ewing, his brother-in-law, to advance the brigades of Brig. Gen. John M. Corse and Col. John M. Loomis. These were only two of the nine brigades present and available. The initial attack consisted of Corse's 920 men, augmented by a regiment of less than 200 men from Brig. Gen. Joseph Lightburn's brigade of Brig. Gen. Morgan L. Smith's division. Loomis was ordered to advance his brigade on the terrain between the two railroads. This area was not part of the initial assault, and this offensive utilized only 1,100 of the 16,600 available soldiers.[7]

Results/Impact

Sherman's critical decision for a small percentage of his available forces to attack a well-entrenched Confederate position was rather astonishing. Cleburne had perhaps 1,300 soldiers dug in on his line to repel the attack. Sherman would face a growing Rebel force during the day's fighting, yet he failed to take early advantage of his current numbers.[8]

Already rebuked by Grant for his tardiness, Sherman nonetheless did not press the issue. Although Sherman initially ordered him to move out at 5:00 a.m., it was 8:00 a.m. before Corse began to advance. He and his men were soon repulsed. Other lackadaisical attacks by the Union accomplished no real gain in position. Around 10:00 a.m. Sherman received another message from Grant demanding action, something to which Sherman was unaccustomed. By noon the first wave of Union attacks ended unsuccessfully.[9]

Hardee realized the gravity of Cleburne's situation and kept sending him reinforcements, growing the Confederate ranks. Sherman's critical decision to underutilize available manpower brought the Union attack on the Confederate right flank to a virtual standstill. This circumstance would have major consequences for fighting later in the day, forcing Grant to devise a new plan of attack.[10]

Alternate Decision and Scenario

Had Sherman's initial morning attack involved most of his available manpower, he would likely have outmaneuvered and overrun Cleburne. With favorable odds of fifteen to one and Union troops' ability to outflank the enemy, the outcome should not have been in doubt. As Grant expected, sending most or all of Sherman's men on a coordinated attack and flanking movement at dawn on the twenty-fifth could well have overwhelmed Cleburne's troops on Tunnel Hill. Cleburne's excellent defensive position was nonetheless vulnerable to being flanked. Sherman's failure to order an aggressive assault against and around Tunnel Hill wasted time and manpower.[11]

Grant Orders Thomas to Conduct a Demonstration

Situation

By midmorning it was obvious to Grant that Sherman's advance was not moving along as expected. Grant decided to order one of Thomas's divisions under the command of Brig. Gen. Absalom Baird to support Sherman. Sherman, however, replied that he already had more than enough men. While Grant's concern mounted, Maj. Gen. George Thomas, commander of the Army of the Cumberland, seemed doomed to a secondary role in the battle. Grant had a low opinion of that army's performance at the Battle of Chickamauga, and he also thought Thomas was too slow and plodding. Meanwhile, Thomas awaited Grant's orders.[12]

By about 2:30 p.m. it was apparent to many Union commanders that Sherman's assault had failed. Grant realized that he had to act to keep additional reinforcements from reaching Cleburne. Hooker and his divisions were marching from Lookout Mountain after their victory there, and they were under orders to assault Bragg's left flank at Rossville Gap. But as the destroyed bridge across Chattanooga Creek had to be rebuilt, they had not yet arrived. Grant began to feel that a diversionary movement was necessary to regain the momentum.[13]

Options

While Sherman struggled with Cleburne, who was defending the Rebel right flank at Tunnel Hill, Grant had two options. He could support and assist Hooker as he advanced upon the vulnerable Confederate left flank now located at Rossville Gap. On the other hand, Grant could order some kind of diversion to capture the Rebels' attention.[14]

Option 1

With Hooker's success on Lookout Mountain and Bragg's critical decision to abandon it, Hooker was already en route to Rossville Gap. Capturing the gap would prevent Confederate retreat at that location, and Hooker's three divisions could begin to roll up Bragg's left flank. Reinforcing Hooker's planned attack on Bragg's left flank would potentially be more effective than Sherman's hitherto-failed assault at Tunnel Hill. A portion of Thomas's army could be tasked with supporting Hooker.[15]

Option 2

Some kind of diversionary movement might distract the Rebels from reinforcing their right flank at Tunnel Hill. A demonstration or advance to the bottom of Missionary Ridge would certainly capture Bragg's and his army's attention. The Confederates would be forced to prepare for an assault, potentially taking some of the pressure off of Sherman.[16]

Decision

Grant made the critical decision to order Thomas's Army of the Cumberland, all four divisions' worth, to advance to the foot of Missionary Ridge as a diversionary movement or demonstration. While concerned over the delay of Hooker, Thomas did not agree with Grant's orders, fearing the unnecessary loss of his men. Thomas assumed Hooker would arrive in due time and assault Bragg's new left flank at Rossville Gap. However, Grant had made up his mind and ordered a demonstration on the Rebel line at the base of the ridge.[17]

Results/Impact

Around 4:00 p.m. Thomas's four divisions began their advance. Safely positioned in timber, these soldiers knew that the last three hundred to seven hundred yards to the base of the ridge were completely cleared. Thus the divisions would be exposed to galling Confederate fire. However, the advance of some twenty-three thousand Union soldiers in near-perfect alignment would have been a daunting sight for the Rebel soldiers. More importantly, Confederate commanders quickly fixated on this movement. As the Union advance continued, Rebel defenders began deserting their line at Missionary Ridge's base and scrambling up to their line at its top. The Federal lines quickly advanced into the Confederate rifle pits and entrenchments, killing, wounding, and capturing the remaining men. Grant's order to advance had paid off. However, attacking the center of Bragg's line had never been Grant's plan. The flanks were supposed to be rolled up first by Sherman on the right, and then with Hooker's help on the Confederate left.[18]

Alternate Decisions and Scenarios

Had Grant reinforced Hooker with some of Thomas's men, what might have transpired? Although construction of a new bridge over Chattanooga Creek delayed Hooker, he would likely have reached Rossville Gap in a few hours. With Sherman effectively stymied on Bragg's right flank, the Rebel left flank appeared vulnerable. A reinforced Hooker would have been virtually unstoppable as he advanced northeast along Missionary Ridge. He might have accomplished on Bragg's left flank what Sherman was supposed to have accomplished on Bragg's right flank. The addition of some of Thomas's troops could have guaranteed the success of this advance, sweeping Bragg off of Missionary Ridge and opening Chattanooga fully for Grant. The flanking maneuver might well have reduced Grant's casualties. He could have claimed victory without incurring additional losses to Thomas's Army of the Cumberland.[19]

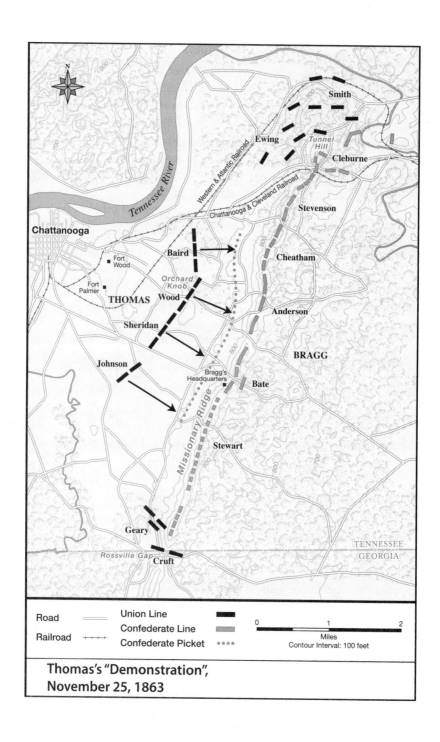

**Thomas's "Demonstration",
November 25, 1863**

Thomas's Troops Decide to Continue the Assault

Situation

Having successfully advanced to the base of Missionary Ridge, the four divisions of Thomas's Army of the Cumberland quickly found themselves in a dilemma. Although in control of the enemy line at the base of the ridge, they quickly discovered their position was untenable. They were receiving fire from Confederates on the ridge above them. Initially, Confederate fire was sporadic; Rebels hesitated to fire on their own men retreating from the base. Once these exhausted men reached the top, their comrades opened fire on the Union soldiers huddled below. The men of Thomas's divisions soon realized they were in a quandary. If they remained at the base of Missionary Ridge, they would be pinned down. If they retreated, many of them would likely be shot in the back. Unfathomably, the least dangerous option appeared to be forging ahead with the assault up the ridge. Yet what were their orders? Even today, this question remains disputed. Some of Thomas's men believed they were to continue assaulting the ridge, while others insisted that the base was as far as they were ordered to advance. In fact, it appears that Grant's orders were for these soldiers to capture the rifle pits at the base and proceed no farther.[20]

Missionary Ridge, Tennessee. Henry Van Ness Boynton, *The National Military Park: Chickamauga and Chattanooga, An Historical Guide, With Maps and Illustrations* (Cincinnati: Robert Clark and Company, 1895), 135.

Options

Thomas's men now had three options: They could dig in and try to protect their position at the base of the ridge. Alternatively, they could retreat. Finally, Thomas's troops could charge up Missionary Ridge and take the fight to the Rebels.[21]

Option 1

Holding their position and resisting Rebel fire was unlikely. While the Confederates manning the rifle pits at the bottom of the ridge were retreating to the crest, other Rebels were doing their best to enfilade the Yankees as they remained at the bottom. Increasing Confederate fire made it dangerous for Thomas's men to stay at the base of Missionary Ridge. However, their orders were to remain there.[22]

Option 2

Retreating would eventually remove Thomas's men from Rebel fire. Yet as they fell back, these Federals would be particularly exposed. The farther away from the base of Missionary Ridge Thomas's soldiers were, the more potential targets they made for Rebel artillery.[23]

Option 3

The final option was to escape the enfilading fire by continuing the assault up Missionary Ridge. As unlikely as this option initially seemed, it quickly made sense. It also appeared that, due to variations in the terrain, the Yankees could evade some of the Rebel cross fire while climbing.[24]

Decision

In one of the most controversial actions of the Civil War, individual Union units began climbing Missionary Ridge.

Results/Impact

It was clear that remaining at the bottom of the ridge was simply too dangerous. In many cases, advancing upward provided cover from Confederate fire. While some commanders received and followed orders to fall back and remain at the base, others climbed on. Regimental, brigade, and division commanders collectively made the critical decision to continue the assault. Grant was initially furious at what he considered disobedience of his orders.

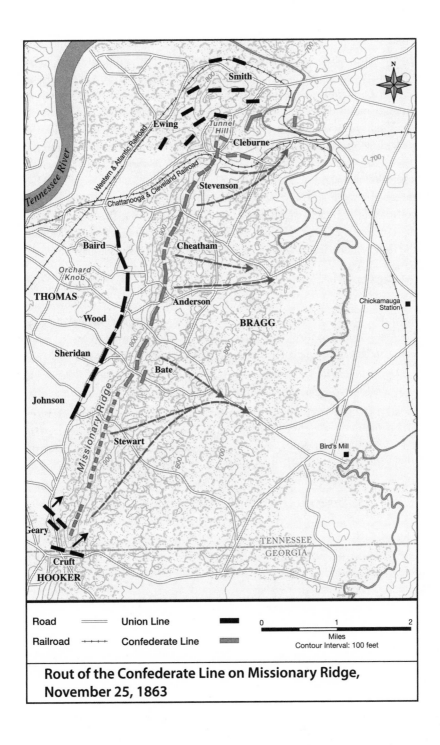

Rout of the Confederate Line on Missionary Ridge, November 25, 1863

However, and unusually, Grant ordered the capture of the Confederate rifle pits and entrenchments at Missionary Ridge's base without thinking through the consequences. While an excellent diversion, leaving Thomas's men in harm's way with little recourse was not an acceptable solution. Nonetheless, Grant demanded to know who ordered the assault up the ridge.[25]

Thomas's men regrouped just below the crest for a final assault. With the Rebel line positioned on the much less effective topographical crest, not the more easily defended military crest, Union units re-formed and then boldly advanced over the top and attacked the thin Rebel line. This unauthorized movement captured the crest of Missionary Ridge. Moreover, it caused the collapse of the entire Confederate defense at Chattanooga. This was a tremendous victory for Grant, Thomas, and the war-weary United States. Overrun, the Confederates immediately began retreating toward Chickamauga Station, Ringgold, and eventually Dalton.[26]

Disobeying Grant's orders to continue the assault was the only reasonable solution to the problem of relief from Confederate fire. Many individuals took credit for the decision to advance upward, and many of them bragged of being the first to arrive at the crest. Collective credit must be given to brave Union commanders and soldiers for their tough decision and resulting victory.[27]

Alternate Decision and Scenario

What if the four divisions of Thomas's army had not continued to advance? Grant might have ordered artillery support to keep the Rebels atop Missionary Ridge heads down, thus interfering with their shelling and firing on Thomas's men. Perhaps furious retrenching of the Confederate line at the bottom of the ridge might have supplied some protection. For the Union soldiers, retreating would most likely have resulted in many more casualties and yielding the ground Thomas's men had just occupied. [28]

CHAPTER 5

POST-BATTLE, NOVEMBER 25–27, 1863

The fighting atop Missionary Ridge quickly turned into a rout of Bragg's army. Hooker was finally able to bridge Chattanooga Creek, and his divisions advanced up Missionary Ridge from Rossville Gap, capturing many remaining Rebels. Bragg's army was soon in full retreat. Confederate soldiers passed through Chickamauga Station, heading southeast toward Ringgold and then Dalton. While Bragg's men were vulnerable to Union pursuit, his supply wagons and remaining artillery were especially at risk.

Bragg Orders Cleburne to Protect the Confederate Retreat

Situation

The Confederacy's disastrous loss of Missionary Ridge was an enormous blow to its war effort. For the Union to capitalize on this victory, its high command needed to aggressively pursue Bragg's army and try to capture or destroy it. Since the seizure of Missionary Ridge's crest had been a surprise, there had been no preplanning for this contingency. By this time darkness had fallen over the battlefield, complicating the Union's response but aiding the Rebels' escape.[1]

Maj. Gen. Philip Sheridan initiated an immediate pursuit. However, the lack of visibility and his inability to enforce command made the pursuit too difficult to maintain. Normally, Grant would have been in favor of a vigorous pursuit. But in this instance he was caught in a dilemma: although expecting victory, he was not prepared for how it happened. Also, now that Grant was free from the siege, he felt he should turn his attention to Maj. Gen. Ambrose E. Burnside and his Ninth Corps at Knoxville. Burnside had been clamoring for relief from Longstreet's divisions there for days, and the Lincoln administration had been insisting that Grant provide assistance. Union pursuit was thus compromised.[2]

Grant sorted out his plan by morning. He ordered Sherman to march to Knoxville to reinforce Burnside, and he sent Thomas to pursue what was left of Bragg's army. Meanwhile, the Rebels retreated through Chickamauga Station farther south. Hooker ordered a reconnaissance from his position. In turn, Thomas directed him to begin a pursuit. By the time meaningful Union pursuit commenced, the remnants of the Confederate army were across Chickamauga Creek and in full retreat. Grant was furious at the delay.[3]

Having suffered a serious defeat, General Bragg knew that he might also lose his entire army if he could not protect it from the trailing Federal pursuits. While the exhausted Rebels continued their retreat some fifteen miles farther south to Dalton, Bragg had to stave off any enemy pursuit. He desperately needed to save the artillery and supply wagons following the Confederate infantry.[4]

Options

Two options were available to Bragg. He could hope each unit could retreat southward on its own past Ringgold and on to Dalton. His other choice was to devise some kind of protection for the retreating troops.[5]

Option 1

In the midst of a Confederate disaster, Bragg could have ordered his various disorganized brigades and divisions to find their way toward Ringgold, Dalton, and hopefully sanctuary on their own. This option would result in Bragg's individual units, with their wagons and artillery, being strung out and vulnerable to Yankee capture.[6]

Option 2

Bragg could order a specific command to protect his retreat until his army could escape. He also knew that his wagons and remaining artillery had to be protected so that they would be available for future battles.[7]

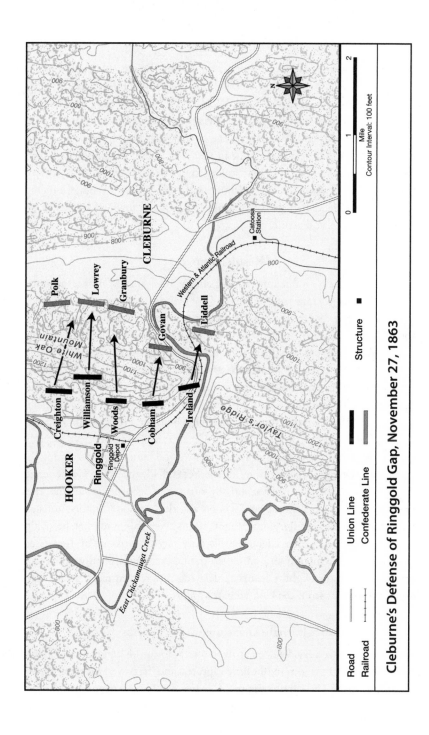

Cleburne's Defense of Ringgold Gap, November 27, 1863

Road
Railroad

Union Line
Confederate Line

Structure

Mile
Contour Interval: 100 feet

Decision

Late on the evening of November 25, Bragg made the critical decision to use Cleburne's division as the Confederate rear guard for Hardee's corps. Brig. Gen. Bragg also assigned Maj. Gen. W. H. T. Walker's division, commanded by Brig. Gen. States Rights Gist, to be the rear guard for Breckinridge's corps. Both units performed adequately on the twenty-sixth, but by evening, Gist's men were too exhausted to continue in that role. Therefore, Bragg appointed Cleburne's division the sole rear guard from the twenty-seventh onward. More specifically, early on the morning of the November 27, Bragg ordered Cleburne to defend Ringgold Gap, just south of the town of Ringgold, to allow the wagons and artillery to escape.[8]

Results/Impact

Cleburne's division retained its fighting ability; it was one of only a few units along Missionary Ridge the Yankees had not overrun. Cleburne had no choice but to accept this assignment. Yet he refused to order his exhausted men across the cold, deep Chickamauga Creek that night, fearing they would catch pneumonia. The troops crossed the next morning under better conditions.[9]

The critical decision for Cleburne and his division to protect the Confederate retreat from the twenty-seventh forward saved the army from further destruction. To stave off Union pursuit, Cleburne fortified Ringgold Gap, just south of the town of Ringgold, through which the Western and Atlantic Railroad and the South Chickamauga Creek ran. Cleburne cleverly positioned his men on both sides of the gap and Col. Daniel Govan's (Liddell's) brigade in the gap in preparation for the Federal advance. The Confederate dispositions caught Hooker's troops by surprise. Cleburne's men first ambushed and then held off repeated Union assaults. At noon Hardee notified Cleburne that the artillery and wagon trains were safe and that he could retreat. Bragg's assigning Cleburne this duty saved the Army of Tennessee from further destruction and preserved the desperately needed wagons and artillery for another fight. Cleburne's delaying action eventually earned him an official thanks from the Confederate Congress.[10]

Alternate Decisions and Scenarios

Had Bragg allowed his defeated army to retreat toward Ringgold and Dalton on its own, Union troops might have captured and destroyed many of his divisions, artillery, and supply wagons. This loss would have been catastrophic, encompassing much of Bragg's army.[11]

CHAPTER 6

CONCLUSION

The campaign and battle for Chattanooga resulted in a huge victory for Grant, Lincoln, and the Union. Unfortunately for the Confederacy, the fighting for the city was nothing short of a disaster. Several conclusions can be drawn from the critical decisions taken by both sides.

Three of the nineteen critical decisions were made at the national level—two by President Abraham Lincoln for the Union, and one by President Jefferson Davis for the Confederacy. Lincoln sent reinforcements from the Eastern Theater (organizational decision) and consolidated the three Western Theater departments into one, commanded by Maj. Gen. Ulysses S. Grant (organizational decision). Davis's decision kept Gen. Braxton Bragg in command of the Army of Tennessee despite his subordinates' many requests for his removal (personnel decision).

Once Maj. Gen. Ulysses S. Grant was placed in command of the newly formed Military Division of the Mississippi, he made five critical decisions at the departmental level, shaping the Battle of Chattanooga's outcome. Grant's critical decisions were: ordering the opening of the "Cracker Line" (logistical decision), directing Maj. Gen. William T. Sherman to march directly to Chattanooga (organizational), sending Sherman to roll up the Confederate right flank (tactical decision), ordering Thomas to make a reconnaissance in force to forestall a possible Confederate retreat (tactical decision), and ordering a demonstration to the base of Missionary Ridge to ease pressure on Sherman (tactical decision).

At the army level, Gen. Braxton Bragg made the following six critical decisions: not aggressively pursuing the retreating Union army after the Battle of Chickamauga (tactical decision), continuing to defend poorly designated lines (tactical decision), dispatching Lieut. Gen. James Longstreet to Knoxville (organizational and personnel decisions), ordering Maj. Gen. Patrick Cleburne to protect the Confederate right flank at Tunnel Hill (tactical decision), ordering Lookout Mountain to be abandoned (tactical decision), and ordering Cleburne to protect the Rebel rear as it retreated to Dalton (tactical decision). Also at the army level, Maj. Gen. William T. Sherman made two critical decisions. First, he canceled the attack on Tunnel Hill and ordered his men to entrench (tactical decision). The next day, he failed to utilize all the brigades assigned to him to attack and/or outflank Cleburne at Tunnel Hill (tactical decision). Two critical decisions were made at the corps level. Lieut. Gen. James Longstreet did not adequately fortify the Wauhatchie Valley against the potential Union advance (tactical decision), and Maj. Gen. John Breckinridge located the Confederate line atop Missionary Ridge along the topographical crest (tactical decision). Finally, one critical decision was made jointly at the Union company/regimental/brigade/division levels—a host of commanders apparently disobeyed orders and continued advancing to the crest of Missionary Ridge (tactical decision).

Of the six types of critical decisions, the Union early on made the strategic critical decision to capture and retain Chattanooga. This decision defined the entire campaign and war, and so it is not counted per se. Thirteen tactical critical decisions were made during the campaign, far and away the most numerous variety. The fighting for Chattanooga also witnessed four organizational critical decisions, no operational critical decisions, and one logistical critical decision. Finally, while two personnel decisions were reached, note that I group Bragg's ordering Longstreet to Knoxville in two categories. Bragg used the chance to reorganize his army to send Longstreet away, making this an organizational and personnel decision.

Several themes appear once the situation was established for the Battle of Chattanooga. First, in order to eliminate senior officers critical of his management of the Army of Tennessee, Bragg systematically dispersed units needed to maintain his semi-siege. In contrast, Grant systematically increased his numbers in preparation for a breakout. Bragg's failure to adequately fortify the crest of Missionary Ridge contributed to his self-inflicted manpower shortage.

Both sides suffered setbacks when corps commanders failed to carry out their assignments. Longstreet's inadequate fortification of the Wauhatchie Valley was insubordination, and Bragg and the Confederate high command had every right to be disgusted. Longstreet's disobedience of orders and sulking contributed to the opening of the Union "Cracker Line," which eventually resulted in offensive operations and victory. By not using all of his resources to aggressively attack Tunnel Hill, Sherman ruined Grant's entire plan of battle.

Cleburne provided some of the Confederacy's bright spots. On Bragg's orders, Cleburne and his available men kept the Federals from rolling up the Confederate right flank at Tunnel Hill. Moreover, Cleburne's defense of the Confederate retreat was nothing short of brilliant, allowing the Army of Tennessee to fight another day.

Union statistics for the fighting at Chattanooga were 753 killed, 4,722 wounded, and 349 missing, for a total of 5,824 casualties. The soldiers present for duty numbered 102,903; approximately 56,000 of these were actually engaged in the fighting. Thus the Union suffered a 10 percent loss of men. While this is certainly significant, the Federal army had a large pool of manpower to provide additional recruits. And this late in the Civil War, the benefits of the victory meant that the loss was not particularly large.[1]

The direct results of the Battle of Chattanooga were favorable for the Union cause. Having forced the enemy out of the city, the Union gained another large supply depot deeper within the Confederacy. Federal supply trains now ran all the way into Chattanooga. At the same time, the Confederacy could no longer move troops and supplies through Chattanooga by rail. Longstreet's two divisions had reached near the city by taking trains from Richmond through Atlanta, and this indirect route would now be the norm for the Confederacy. The delivery of troops and supplies was thus further delayed. Most of Tennessee was now held by the Yankees, and necessities were no longer available from much of the Confederate "Heartland." Finally, the Union now had an excellent location from which to launch a campaign even farther into the Deep South and interdict cities, farms, and industries. For those willing to accept it, the Confederacy's demise now seemed likely.[2]

After Bragg's successful retreat south to the Dalton area, the Confederate situation was grim. The Army of Tennessee had suffered considerably, experiencing significant losses of men and supplies. During the retreat the Rebels' food- and supply-laden warehouses at Chickamauga Station were burned, much to the disgust of soldiers whose food and supplies had been inadequate for months. Bragg estimated that his army had lost thirty-eight pieces of field artillery and two 24-pound siege guns abandoned at Chickamauga Station, where their carriages were burned. Casualties were listed as 361 killed, 2,180 wounded, and 4,146 missing (likely captured), for a total of 6,687. The estimate of approximately 46,000 Rebels present for the final days of the battle would place Bragg's casualties at roughly 13.5 percent. While this figure doesn't seem particularly high, it was virtually impossible to provide replacements. Yankees captured some 6,175 small arms, including Enfield muskets imported from England, on the battlefield. An additional unknown number of rifled muskets and other fighting accoutrements were lost or discarded during the retreat, as well as many invaluable horses, mules, and wagons. These would also be extremely difficult to replace due to their dwindling availability in the Confederacy. Though in poor condition, the Rebel supply line, the Western and Atlantic Railroad, was fortunately available to deliver any existing supplies from Atlanta to Dalton.[3]

Bragg finally realized that he could no longer effectively command and offered his resignation, which was accepted on November 30. Lieut. Gen. William J. Hardee was appointed interim commander, but he would only accept the position until a permanent commander was named. On December 27 Gen. Joseph E. Johnston, the new commander, arrived at Dalton. Many welcomed the change, but what it would mean for the next year's fighting remained to be seen.[4]

Looking forward in Civil War history, several events took advantage of the Union victory at Chattanooga. President Lincoln believed that in Grant he had finally found a fighting general who could command all of the Union armies, properly coordinate their efforts, defeat the various Confederate forces, and end the war. After observing Grant manage the three departments in the Military Division of the Mississippi and complete his third successful campaign with the Battle of Chattanooga, Lincoln petitioned Congress to reestablish the rank of lieutenant general. It had been originally designated for George Washington, and Maj. Gen. Winfield Scott had held it as a brevet. Lincoln successfully nominated Grant to the position as general-in-chief of all Union armies.[5]

Sherman wanted Grant to remain in the Western Theater. However, in part due to politics, Grant ultimately oversaw Union fighting in the Eastern Theater, while monitoring the other armies. Grant assigned Sherman to command the Military Division of the Mississippi in his absence. Sherman then prepared for a campaign to move south into northern Georgia. According to Grant's orders, he was to follow Johnston's Army of Tennessee and render it ineffective. Sherman's advance into northern Georgia resulted in what is now designated the Atlanta Campaign.[6]

After many months of fighting Sherman gave up on capturing the Army of Tennessee, now under the command of Gen. John B. Hood. He then focused on Atlanta, capturing it on September 2, 1864. Sherman launched his March to the Sea shortly thereafter, presenting Lincoln with the city of

Savannah as a Christmas present, and then advancing north to join Grant's troops surrounding Petersburg. Before Sherman and his armies could rejoin Grant, the latter overran Lee's Army of Northern Virginia after nine months' siege at Petersburg. Grant pursued the Confederate forces to Appomattox Court House, where Lee surrendered on April 9, 1865, effectively ending the American Civil War.[7]

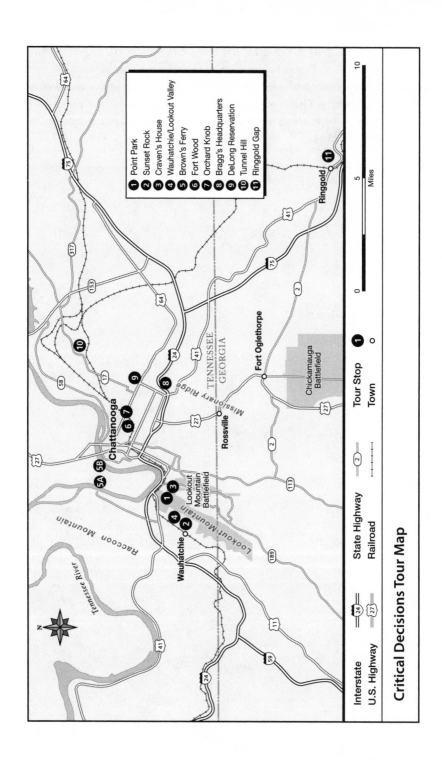

Critical Decisions Tour Map

Legend:
1 Point Park
2 Sunset Rock
3 Craven's House
4 Wauhatchie/Lookout Valley
5 Brown's Ferry
6 Fort Wood
7 Orchard Knob
8 Bragg's Headquarters
9 DeLong Reservation
10 Tunnel Hill
11 Ringgold Gap

Interstate
U.S. Highway
State Highway
Railroad

Tour Stop
Town

Raccoon Mountain
Tennessee River
Lookout Mountain
Lookout Mountain Battlefield
Wauhatchie
Chattanooga
Missionary Ridge
Rossville
Fort Oglethorpe
Chickamauga Battlefield
Ringgold
TENNESSEE
GEORGIA

Miles
0 5 10

APPENDIX I

DRIVING TOUR OF THE CRITICAL DECISIONS OF THE BATTLE OF CHATTANOOGA

This is a driving tour of some of the sites where critical decisions of the Battle of Chattanooga were made. In some cases, you will be directed to a nearby area rather than the exact location of a decision. What follows is *not* a traditional tour of the battle. (Those can be found elsewhere. One highly recommended title is Matt Spruill's *Storming the Heights: A Guide to the Battle of Chattanooga*, published by the University of Tennessee Press in 2003.) To eliminate repetitive driving, this tour departs from the battle's chronology. Many of the stops review multiple critical decisions where they were made and where they were executed.

Please keep your safety in mind as you drive, park, leave your vehicle, walk, and return to your vehicle. Parking may be tricky in certain locations. Note that tour directions precede each stop.

If you are familiar with Chattanooga-area roads, drive to the top of Lookout Mountain, and proceed to Point Park. Otherwise, begin this tour from Exit 178 off of I-24 (either direction). Exit, and follow the signs to Broad Street, which is also US Highway 41 North. Turn left (south) on Broad Street (US 41 North). Follow the signs to Lookout Mountain, and drive 2.3 miles to the intersection with Tennessee Highway 148. A sign indicates Ruby Falls and Lookout Mountain to the left. Turn left (south) onto Highway 148, and continue. In 0.2 mile, turn left again, and proceed up Lookout Mountain for 2.2 miles to the intersection with East Brow Road. Turn right (north) onto East Brow Road, and drive 1.1 miles to Point Park and the National Park Service visitor center. Park your vehicle nearby (parking extends past the visitor

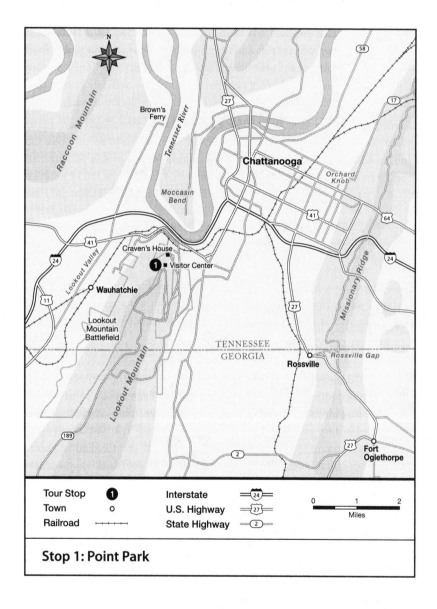

Stop 1: Point Park

center and around it). Walk to the park entrance, pay the entrance fee, and walk through the castle-like entrance into Point Park. Walk along the flag-stone path about 220 yards, passing Corput's Cherokee Georgia Artillery and Garrity's Alabama Battery. Follow the sign to the Ochs Memorial Observatory and Overlook. At the stone building, which is the observatory, walk to the waist-high wall. You will have a sweeping view of the area. From your left (west) to right (east), note the locations of Lookout Valley and Wauhatchie, the Tennessee River, Brown's Ferry, Moccasin Bend, Chattanooga in front, and Missionary Ridge to your right.

Stop 1—Lookout Mountain/Point Park

Critical Decisions: (1) Bragg Orders a Limited Pursuit of Rosecrans After the Battle of Chickamauga, (3) Lincoln Orders the Eleventh and Twelfth Corps to Chattanooga, (4) Davis Decides to Keep Bragg in Command of the Army of Tennessee, (5) Lincoln Decides to Consolidate the Three Western Departments

This stop begins a tour of the critical decisions of the Battle of Chattanooga. Before continuing, let's review the critical decisions made elsewhere. Critical Decision 1 involved Bragg's ordering a limited pursuit of Rosecrans after the Battle of Chickamauga. The fighting at Chickamauga occurred less than ten miles south of your location as the crow flies. This limited pursuit allowed Rosecrans's army to safely retreat into the environs of Chattanooga and quickly establish a solid defensive ring around the city. Bragg lost the chance to capture large parts of the Army of the Cumberland or force its retreat back out of Chattanooga. As a result, his only option was to establish a siege confining the Yankees.

Report of Col. Alfred J. Vaughan Jr., CSA, Acting Commander, Smith's Brigade, Cheatham's Division, Polk's Corps, Army of Tennessee

After two days of grand and magnificent fighting the enemy was completely routed and victory perched on the Confederate banner; but, alas! Its fruits were lost by the tardy movements of the army in following up the victory.[1]

Narrative of Pvt. W. M. Pollard, CSA, Company D, First Tennessee Infantry, Smith's Brigade, Cheatham's Division, Polk's Corps, Army of Tennessee

[Bragg] lost the opportunity of a life time [*sic*]. [2]

Lincoln made Critical Decision 3, ordering the Eleventh and Twelfth Corps to Chattanooga, some six hundred miles away in Washington, DC. This was the Union's initial attempt to reinforce the Army of the Cumberland. Although Lincoln had to be persuaded to act, the eventual addition of over fourteen thousand soldiers was a key element in the eventual Union victory at Chattanooga.

Message from Maj. Gen. Henry Halleck, USA, to Maj. Gen. William Rosecrans

War Department
Washington, September 24, 1863 2.30 a.m.
Major General Rosecrans
Chattanooga, Tenn.:

In addition to the expected assistance to you from Burnside, Hurlbut, and Sherman, 14,000 or 15,000 men from here will be in Nashville in about seven days. The Government deems it very important that Chattanooga be held till re-enforcements arrive.

H. Halleck
General-in-Chief[3]

Critical Decision 4 was President Jefferson Davis's choice to keep Gen. Braxton Bragg in command of the Army of Tennessee. It was quite unusual for a general to be removed from overall command after a victory. But in this situation, some subordinate commanders were continuing to call for Bragg's removal. Bragg had lost the officers' confidence, and Davis should have long since recognized the problem and resolved it. Leaving Bragg in command and supporting his elimination or transfer of officers who criticized him diverted his focus from the situation at and around Chattanooga.

Narrative of Thomas L. Connelly

By October 14 he [Bragg] was committed to the idea of completely revamping his command structure to eliminate opposition. Practically every major officer who had taken part would be driven from the army. Bragg seemed to believe that Davis had given him carte blanche for such a step. In a conversation with [Brig. Gen. St. John R.] Liddell, he insisted that Davis had authorized him to relieve "any and every officer" who did not sustain him. . . . In short, Davis seemed to believe little if any of the trouble was Bragg's fault.[4]

Lincoln made Critical Decision 5, appointing U. S. Grant commander of the Military Division of the Mississippi and consolidating authority in the Western Theater, in Washington, DC, as well. For the first time there was a unified command in the West under a successful general. Grant would soon prove himself worthy of the appointment, although a little of "Grant's luck" wouldn't hurt.

General Orders No. 337

War Department
Adjutant-Generals [*sic*] office
Washington, D.C., October 16, 1863
General Orders
No. 337

 I. By direction of the President of the United States the Departments of the Ohio, of the Cumberland, and of the Tennessee will constitute the Military Division of the Mississippi.

 II. Maj. Gen. U. S. Grant, U.S. Army is placed in command of the Military Division of the Mississippi, headquarters in the field.

 III. Maj. Gen. Rosecrans, U.S. Volunteers, is relieved from the command of the Department and Army of the Cumberland. Maj. Gen. G. H. Thomas is hereby assigned to that command.

 By order of the Secretary of War:

E. D. Townsend
Assistant Adjutant General[5]

Walk back to the visitor center, and explore it if open.

When you are finished viewing the visitor center, return to your vehicle. Leave the parking area by driving around the visitor center, then turn right to rejoin East Brow Road, now heading south. Drive one block to Richardson Street, and turn hard right (northwest) onto it. Drive one long block on Richardson Street to the intersection with West Brow Road. Turn left (south-southwest), and continue 0.8 mile along West Brow Road to the Sunset Rock parking area. Park, leave your vehicle, and follow the short trail to Sunset Rock. For your safety please stay on the trail, and watch your footing.

Stop Two—Sunset Rock

Critical Decisions: (6) Grant Orders the "Cracker Line" Opened, (7) Longstreet Decides Not to Fortify Lookout Valley

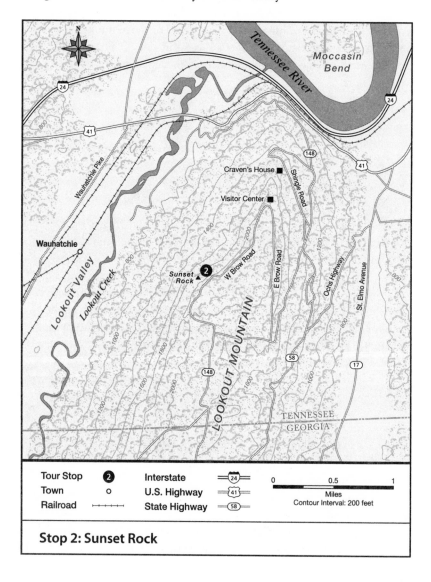

Stop 2: Sunset Rock

With Critical Decision 7, Longstreet opted not to fortify Lookout Valley. The valley below is Lookout Valley, and the area immediately below is Wauhatchie. There, Longstreet halfheartedly tried to end Union control of Lookout Valley with an attack on an isolated force under the command of Brig. Gen. John Geary. You will visit Wauhatchie at Stop 4. As you can see, this valley is a natural transportation route to and from Chattanooga, by both water and land. It was crucial for the Union supply line that the valley remain in Union possession. As a result, Grant made Critical Decision 6 to open the "Cracker Line." Rebel control of this valley forced the initial Union line of supply to wind many miles to the north to avoid Confederate interdiction. But even that was not guaranteed. Maj. Gen. Joseph Wheeler's raid on the alternate route quickly showed its weakness, in addition to its much longer length.

Longstreet had decided that Federal reinforcements, rather than marching up Lookout Valley, would ascend Lookout Mountain south of the Confederate position on its north end. Therefore, he did not adequately protect Lookout Valley from Federal invasion. Nor did Longstreet protect the valley from the eventuality of a reestablished Union supply line.

Report of Lt. Gen. James Longstreet, CSA, Commanding Longstreet's Corps, Army of Northern Virginia

Headquarters
October 27, 1863
Col. George William Brent
Assistant-Adjutant-General

Colonel: Your note of today is received. The enemy designs seem to be to occupy this bank of the river for the purpose of shortening his line of communication and possibly for the purpose of creating a diversion near the point of Lookout Mountain, while he moves a heavier force up to occupy the mountain, via Johnson's Crook [many miles south]. The latter move and object seems to me to be more important, essential indeed, than any such partial move as his present one.[6]

This critical decision, and Grant's desire to open this same supply line, would seriously harm Confederate chances of containing the bottled-up Union forces in Chattanooga.

Return to your vehicle, depart the Sunset Rock parking area, and turn right (south-southwest) back onto the West Brow Road. Continue winding back 0.5 mile to a fountain. Turn left (east) onto Scenic Highway 148, and continue 1.5 miles, descending from the top of Lookout Mountain and turning north. At the Cravens House Road, turn left onto it, and continue 0.6 mile to the Craven's House parking lot. Leave your vehicle, walk to the house, stand near it, and look in all directions.

Stop 3—The Craven's House

Critical Decision 15: Bragg Decides to Abandon Lookout Mountain

Surprisingly, Lookout Mountain was not critical to either side. The Union's concern was the supply line through Lookout Valley and the Tennessee River, while the Confederate goal was blocking that supply line. Rebel artillerymen originally believed their location was ideal. However, they were unable to fire effectively into either Lookout Valley or Chattanooga. Grant saw little value in possessing Lookout Mountain, preferring to attack the Confederate right flank on Missionary Ridge when he was able. The inability to get all Federal units across the Tennessee River left Hooker with three divisions at his disposal. With this larger-than-expected force, he saw an opportunity to strike Rebel forces on Lookout Mountain and retake it. Braxton Bragg finally realized the peril facing his weak right flank on Missionary Ridge while Hooker attacked Lookout Mountain. Thus the Confederate general made Critical Decision 15, abandoning Lookout Mountain on November 24. The assaults by Hooker's soldiers culminated here at the Craven's House. While fighting their way up the mountain, these troops were temporarily repulsed Rebels under the command of Brig. Gen. Edward C. Walthall.

Report of Lt. Col. A. J. Jones, CSA, Commanding Twenty-seventh Mississippi, Walthall's Brigade, Cheatham's Division, Hardee's Corps, Army of Tennessee

I was ordered by General Walthall to rally my men on a little ridge running up and down the mountain, 300 or 400 yards from our first position, which I did, and where the men fought most bravely until, seeing we were flanked, or nearly so, by such an overwhelming force, I ordered [them] to fall back; but General Walthall immediately ordered me to hold that point, and I rallied as many men as I could, but in one or two minutes the enemy pointed their guns over logs and rocks within 8 or 10 paces of us, and I ordered to fall back again, and in doing which many, compared with our numbers, were shot down. One or two unsuccessful attempts were made to rally, but the incessant shower of shell and shot from the enemy's batteries and the rush of their heavy force of infantry gave no time for doing so until we had passed around the point of the mountain several hundred yards south of the Craven [*sic*] House.[7]

The Rebel forces on Lookout Mountain were no match for Hooker's beefed-up command. Confederates put up a good fight here around the Craven's House, but they were outmatched. Regardless, Bragg had decided to reinforce his right at the expense of his left on Lookout Mountain.

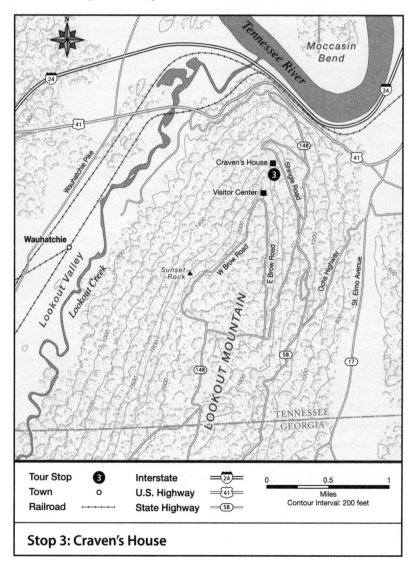

Tour Stop	●	Interstate	24	0	0.5	1
Town	○	U.S. Highway	41	Miles		
Railroad	+++	State Highway	58	Contour Interval: 200 feet		

Stop 3: Craven's House

> **Headquarters, Army of Tennessee, November 24, 2:30 p.m.,**
> **Maj. Gen. C. L. Stevenson, [CSA], Lookout Mountain**
>
> General: The general commanding instructs me to say that you will withdraw your command from the mountain to this side [east] of Chickamauga Creek, destroying the bridges behind. Fight the enemy as you retire. The thickness of the fog will enable you to retire, it is hoped, without much difficulty.[8]

Return to your vehicle, depart the Craven's parking lot, turn left, and drive 1.1 miles to Scenic Highway 148. Turn sharply left (north) onto Highway 148, and continue 0.7 mile to the intersection with Tennessee Highway 318. Turn left (west) onto Highway 318, and continue 0.5 mile to Alford Hill Road on your right. Turn right (north) onto Alford Hill Road, and continue 0.1 mile to the intersection with US Highway 41, Cummings Parkway. Turn left (west) onto US 41, and continue 0.9 mile to the first large intersection with a stoplight. The road to the right is the Brown's Ferry Road, and the road to the left is the Wauhatchie Pike. Turn left (southwest) onto the Wauhatchie Pike, and continue 0.8 mile to the New York monument on your right (northwest). Park safely, leave your vehicle, and face north.

Stop 4—Wauhatchie/Lookout Valley

Critical Decision 7: Longstreet Decides Not to Fortify Lookout Valley

The Battle of Wauhatchie was the result of Longstreet's critical decision not to fortify Lookout Valley, despite Bragg's direct orders. This stop is associated with Longstreet's choice, and you observed this area from Sunset Rock. Faced with Union reinforcements under Hooker marching toward Chattanooga, Longstreet unwisely ordered a nighttime attack on John Geary's lone division encamped at Wauhatchie, several miles from Brown's Ferry. Thus exposed, Geary's men made an excellent target for a Rebel attack. However, Longstreet's effort was too little too late. Most of Hooker's men had already reached Brown's Ferry. After withstanding a sharp attack in which more of Longstreet's soldiers temporarily stopped them from receiving assistance, Geary's men fought off the Confederates until Hooker's troops reinforced them. The Federal survivors were safe. Longstreet had failed to carry out his orders to occupy Lookout Valley and block the Union line of supply.

Report of Brig. Gen. John W. Geary, USA, Commanding Second Division, Twelfth Corps, Army of the Potomac

We resumed the march at 5 o'clock in the morning of the 28th, and by way of Running Waters and Whiteside's, reached Wauhatchie at 4.30 p.m. . . . I ordered the command to bivouac upon their arms, with cartridge boxes on, and placed my guns on a knob about 30 yards to the left of the railroad and immediately to the left of Rowden's house so that they could command either of the cardinal points.[9]

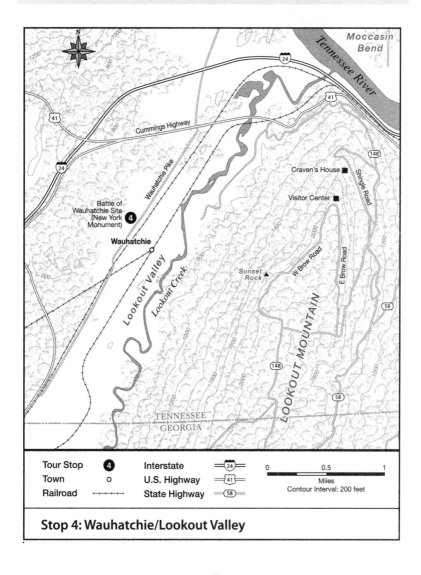

Stop 4: Wauhatchie/Lookout Valley

Report of Col. John Bratton, CSA, Commanding Jenkins's Brigade, Hood's Division, Longstreet's Corps, Army of Northern Virginia

The line thus formed advanced without opposition until near a branch, about half a mile from the point at which we entered the Trenton [Wauhatchie] Road. There, after some little picket firing, our skirmishers crossed the branch, and came in sight of the camp of the enemy. . . . immediately threw three regiments—Second Rifles, First and Fifth—upon them. . . . The three regiments had not advanced far before a very heavy fire was developed. . . . I at once ordered up the Sixth from its position in the rear to act as reserve, and put the Hampton Legion in on the right of the Fifth. . . . [We] drove the enemy through their camp and entirely beyond their wagon camp. . . . Our line was, as it were, two sides of a wide-spread V, the Fifth and Hampton Legion on the right, and the Sixth and Palmetto Sharpshooters on the left, the First at the point, Second Rifles on the left behind the railroad. The enemy with his left driven in upon the center, occupied the base. His line of fire at this time was not more than 300 or 400 yards in length, and but from 50 to 150 yards in breadth, the sparkling fire making a splendid pyrotechnic display. . . . At this juncture I received orders to withdraw and move back in good order, as the enemy was pressing in the rear.[10]

Report of Maj. Gen. Joseph Hooker, USA, Commanding Eleventh and Twelfth Corps, Army of the Potomac

. . . The mutterings of heavy musketry fell upon our ears from the direction of Geary. He was fiercely attacked, first his pickets, and soon after his main force, but not before he was in line of battle to receive it. Howard was directed to double-quick his nearest division (Schurz's) to his relief, and before proceeding far a sheet of musketry was thrown on him from the central hills [behind you], but at long range, and inflicted no great injury. This was the first intimation that the enemy was there at all.[11]

The night attack failed, and Hooker eventually reinforced Geary. Longstreet had again failed to to effectively guard the valley.

Bragg remained furious and would soon relieve himself of the recalcitrant Longstreet. However, the critical decision to send Longstreet away would come to haunt Bragg.

Drive back north on Wauhatchie Pike to the intersection with US 41. Drive straight through the intersection and continue north on what is now Brown's Ferry Road. Continue under I-24 North for 2.8 miles. As you travel about 1.7 miles, note the old log building on the left (west) side of the road: this was Brown's Tavern in 1863. After 2.8 miles you will reach a Y in the road with Burgess Road to the left and Brown's Ferry Road to the right. Follow the right branch, Brown's Ferry Road, and park at the end of it. Leave your vehicle, and enter the preserved grounds of the west entrance to Brown's Ferry. Please respect private property.

Stops 5A and 5B—Brown's Ferry

Critical Decision 6: Grant Orders the "Cracker Line" to Be Opened

NOTE: Brown's Ferry has two stops—the accesses to the west and east entrances to the ferry. The American Battlefield Trust has purchased some of the land on the west side of the Tennessee River where the west entrance to Brown's Ferry was located. It will eventually be accessible to the public. Inquire at the Chickamauga and Chattanooga National Military Park Visitor Center for further information (706-866-9241).

Stop 5A—West Access to Brown's Ferry

Chief engineer Brig. Gen. William F. "Baldy" Smith ordered part of Brig. Gen. William Hazen's brigade to float around Moccasin Bend on the Tennessee River and disembark at night at the west end of Brown's Ferry. He did so successfully, and little fighting resulted. Lieutenant Colonel Foy was part of that action.

> ### Report of Lieut. Col. James C. Foy, USA, Commanding Twenty-third Kentucky Infantry, Second Brigade, Third Division, Fourth Corps, Army of the Cumberland
>
> In a few minutes we struck the shore landing a little below the point where the road strikes the river; at this point we had to scramble up a very steep bank, the men forming as soon as they gained a bench of land that runs along the river at this place. As soon as I had about 20 men up the bank we proceeded to the house. I directed Captain Williams with his squad of men to take possession of the house, while I remained outside awaiting the balance of my party. In a few

moments Captain Boden, with the rear squad arrived, when we all proceeded up the road, marching in one squad of 48 men by the front. After proceeding about 500 yards, and as far beyond the crest of the hill as I thought our skirmishers would come, I ordered a halt, and gave the order for the rear rank to hold the guns of the men in the front rank, and to proceed to build breastworks, but the first thing I did was to throw out skirmishers to our front and well to our right. The men took hold of the work with a will, and we soon had a tolerable protection thrown up.[12]

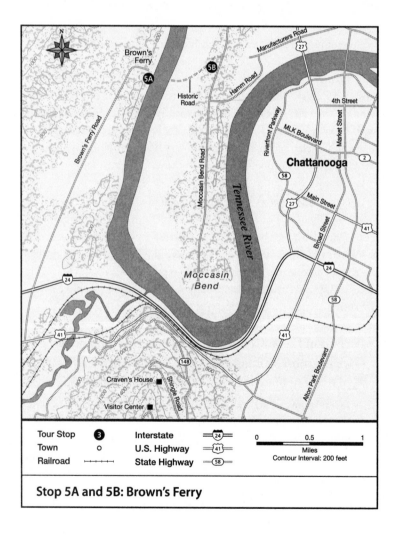

Stop 5A and 5B: Brown's Ferry

Return to your vehicle. Turn around, and drive back (southwest) on Brown's Ferry Road to the intersection with US 41. Turn left (east) onto US 41. Continue east, then south, and then north on US 41, which becomes Broad Street, into Chattanooga, passing under I-24 in about 4.8 miles. After 5.4 miles you will come to the intersection with Main Street. Continue north on Broad Street five blocks to the intersection with West Martin Luther King Boulevard. Continue one block north past West Martin Luther King Boulevard, and turn right (east) onto West Eighth Street. Drive one block east to the intersection with North Market Street. Turn left (north) onto Market Street, and continue eight blocks to the Tennessee River. Cross over the river, and continue 0.1 mile to the intersection with Frazer Avenue to the right and Cherokee Avenue to the left. Turn left (northwest) onto Cherokee Avenue, and drive two blocks to Manufactures Road. Turn left (west) onto Manufactures Road, and continue west-southwest 0.8 mile to a left turn onto Hamm Road. Turn left (south), and follow Hamm Road 0.8 mile to the intersection with Moccasin Bend Road. Turn right (north) onto Moccasin Bend Road, and drive 0.4 mile to the parking lot on the left (west) side of the road labeled Brown's Ferry Federal Road. Park there, leave your vehicle, read the interpretive sign, and walk (if desired) the 0.6 mile trail to the eastern shore of Brown's Ferry. Observe the river and the western side of it where you last stopped. This is the location of Brown's Ferry.

Stop 5B—East Access to Brown's Ferry

Without a reliable line of supply, no army could remain within the confines of Chattanooga. Likewise, additional reinforcements could not be ordered into the city, where there were not enough foodstuffs and feed for the troops and animals. As Rosecrans did before him, Grant knew that this supply problem must be rectified before further action could be taken. Grant's efforts to open the "Cracker Line," rather than attempting to use the present much longer supply line, would allow him to resupply the troops already in Chattanooga, as well as any reinforcements. In so doing, Grant could save time and go on the offensive sooner.

On the night of October 27–28, men from Brig. Gen. William B. Hazen's and Brig. Gen. John B. Turchin's brigades floated down the Tennessee River and around Moccasin Bend, landing across the river. They surprised a small detachment of Confederate pickets and soon established a fortified base of operations. Reinforcements then came directly across the ford. Grant had promptly begun the opening of his most necessary line of supply.

Report of Lieut. Col. James C. Foy, USA, Commanding Twenty-third Kentucky Infantry, Second Brigade, Third Division, Fourth Corps, Army of the Cumberland

I gave directions to each of my captains to take 16 men of their respective squads aboard, making an aggregate of 52 men including myself. We now shoved out and proceeded to cross the river, and float quietly down. I had to proceed slowly and quietly, thinking it would be best not to get too far from the other boats. We arrived opposite the gap without any accident, except the knocking into the river of one man by the top of a tree, where we had run too close to shore. He was picked up by the first following boat.[13]

Promptly, entrenchments were dug and reinforcements brought over. Rebel resistance was futile at this point; Longstreet had failed to protect Lookout Valley from just such an invasion. He would attempt to attack Hooker's force, which would soon be marching up the valley with the botched Battle of Wauhatchie late the following evening.

Here on the night of October 28–29, in conjunction with Grant's critical decision to open the "Cracker Line," Longstreet finally reacted. In compliance with Bragg's orders, he tried to retake Lookout Valley. However, Longstreet's critical decision not to previously ensure control of the valley, and to focus instead on an improbable attack from the south, made him look foolish once again.

Return 0.6 mile back to the parking lot.

Grant's critical decision to open the "Cracker Line" commenced with the successful capture of Brown's Ferry. Brig. Gen. William F. "Baldy" Smith, the chief engineer, proposed this measure. Needless to say, Grant was surprised that action to open the "Cracker Line" had not already begun.

Narrative of Maj. Gen. Ulysses S. Grant, USA, Commmanding, Military Division of the Mississippi

On the morning of the 21st we took the train for the front, reaching Stevenson, Alabama, after dark. Rosecrans was there on his way north. He came into my car and we held a brief interview, in which he described very clearly the situation at Chattanooga, and made some excellent suggestions as to what should be done. My only wonder was that he had not carried them out.[14]

This action helped solidify Grant's critical decision to continue to open the Cracker Line.

Return to your vehicle, and retrace your route on Moccasin Bend Road 0.4 mile south to the intersection with Hamm Road. Turn left (east) onto Hamm Road, and drive 0.2 mile to the future home of the Moccasin Bend National Archaeological District Visitor Center on the right (south). This will eventually provide access to the Tennessee River, near which the expedition to capture Brown's Ferry originated. Continue 0.6 mile back to the intersection with Manufactures Road. Turn right (east) onto Manufactures Road, and continue 0.8 mile to the intersection with Cherokee Avenue. Turn right (southeast) onto Cherokee Avenue, and continue two blocks to the intersection with North Market Street. Turn right (south) onto North Market Street, cross over the Tennessee River, and continue 0.7 mile to Fourth Street. Turn left (east) onto Fourth Street, and continue east and then southeast for 0.6 mile to the intersection with Mabel Street. Turn right (south-southwest) onto Mabel Street, and follow it as it curves left into Fifth Street. Continue past Collins Street (note the Confederate cemetery on your left) one block to the intersection with Palmetto Street. Turn right (south-southwest), and immediately turn left (east-southeast) onto Fort Wood Street. Continue about 0.2 mile to the top of the hill, and park safely. Leave your vehicle, and face east through south as you observe Missionary Ridge in the distance.

Stop 6—Fort Wood

Critical Decisions: (7) Grant Orders Sherman to Proceed Directly to Chattanooga, (10) Grant Orders Sherman to Attack Bragg's Right at Tunnel Hill, (11) Grant Orders Thomas to Conduct a Reconnaissance in Force

Fort Wood was within the Union defenses surrounding Chattanooga. It provided an excellent view of the Rebel defenses on Missionary Ridge.

Grant was eagerly anticipating the arrival of Sherman and his Army of the Tennessee, en route from Memphis. However, Sherman's orders were to rebuild the Memphis and Charleston Railroad, and he moved east toward Chattanooga. Grant thought this detour was taking too much time. Sherman's supply train of wagons was also slowing him down. When Grant realized what was happening, he made Critical Decision 8 to order Sherman to proceed directly to Chattanooga, leaving his wagons behind. Getting Sherman and his army in place sooner rather than later was Grant's wish.

Grant was planning for Sherman to be his key battle commander, so it was not helpful to await Sherman's appearance any longer than necessary. Grant therefore opted to hurry Sherman to Chattanooga with his army and let the cumbersome animals and supply wagons arrive later.

Headquarters, Maj. Gen. Ulysses S. Grant, USA, Commanding Military Division of the Mississippi

CHATTANOOGA, November 13, 1863.
Maj. Gen. W. T. SHERMAN,
Bridgeport, Ala.:

Assemble the Fifteenth Army Corps at Bridgeport, and get ready for moving as soon as possible. Leave directions for your command and come up here yourself. Telegraph when you start, and I will send a horse to Kelley's Ferry for you.[15]

While waiting for Sherman and his men to arrive, Grant made Critical Decision 10, directing Sherman to attack Bragg's right flank at Tunnel Hill and roll up the entire defensive position. This would be the main assault. Other actions would support Sherman. However, Grant allowed Sherman to conduct his own reconnaissance of Tunnel Hill and the Confederate right flank before the attack began.

After making his own reconnaissance, Sherman concurred with Grant's plan. Unfortunately for the two generals, Sherman had failed to accurately ascertain Tunnel Hill's location. When he attacked, he discovered a large gap between his location on Billy Goat Hill and Tunnel Hill. He therefore failed to capture the correct location and was soon met with strong Rebel resistance.

Narrative of Maj. Gen. Ulysses S. Grant, USA, Commanding Military Division of the Mississippi

The plan of battle was for Sherman to attack the enemy's right flank, form a line across it, extend our left over South Chickamauga River so as to threaten or hold the railroad in Bragg's rear, and thus force him either to weaken his lines elsewhere or lose his connection with his base at Chickamauga Station. Hooker was to perform like service on our right. . . . Thomas, with the Army of the Cumberland, occupied the centre, and was to assault while the enemy was engaged with most of his forces on his two flanks.[16]

While at Fort Wood, Grant observed Sherman's difficulties assaulting Tunnel Hill. As a result, he made Critical Decision 11, directing Maj. Gen. George H. Thomas to conduct a reconnaissance in force as a diversion for Bragg, and to establish that Bragg was not retreating.

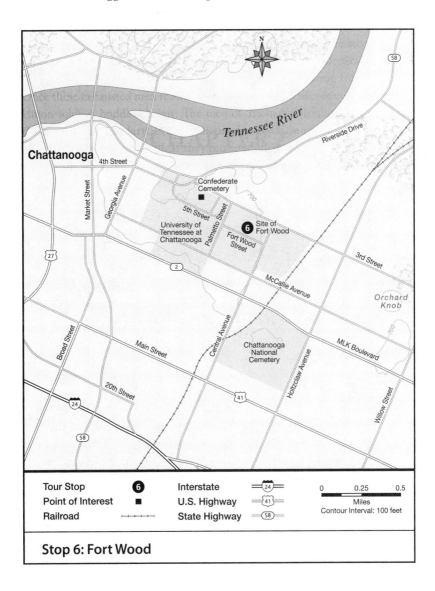

Tour Stop	❻	Interstate	══⟨24⟩══	0	0.25	0.5
Point of Interest	■	U.S. Highway	⟨41⟩		Miles	
Railroad	┼┼┼┼	State Highway	⟨58⟩	Contour Interval: 100 feet		

Stop 6: Fort Wood

Narrative of Maj. Gen. Ulysses S. Grant, USA, Commanding Military Division of the Mississippi

The position occupied by the Army of the Cumberland had been made very strong for defense during the months it had been besieged. The line was about a mile from the town, and extended from Citico Creek, a small stream running near the base of Missionary Ridge and emptying into the Tennessee about two miles below the mouth of the South Chickamauga, on the left, to Chattanooga Creek on the right. All commanding points on the line were well fortified and well equipped with artillery. The important elevations within the line had all been carefully fortified and supplied with a proper armament. Among the elevations so fortified was one to the east of the town, named Fort Wood. It owed its importance chiefly to the fact that it lay between the town and Missionary Ridge, where most of the strength of the enemy was. Fort Wood had in it twenty-two pieces of artillery, most of which would reach the nearer points of the enemy's line. On the morning of the 23d Thomas, according to instructions, moved Granger's corps of two divisions, Sheridan and T. J. Wood commanding, to the foot of Fort Wood, and formed them into line as if going on parade, Sheridan on the right, Wood to the left, extending to or near Citico Creek. Palmer, commanding the 14th corps, held that part of our line facing south and south-west. He supported Sheridan with one division (Baird's), while his other division under Johnson remained in the trenches, under arms, ready to be moved to any point. Howard's corps was moved in rear of the centre. The picket lines were within a few hundred yards of each other. At two o'clock in the afternoon all were ready to advance. By this time the clouds had lifted so that the enemy could see from his elevated position all that was going on. The signal for the advance was given by a booming of cannon from Fort Wood and other points on the line. The rebel pickets were soon driven back upon the main guards, which occupied minor and detached heights between the main ridge and our lines. These too were carried before halting, and before the enemy had time to reinforce their advance guards. But it was not without loss on both sides. This movement secured to us a line fully a mile in advance of the one we occupied in the morning and the one which the enemy had occupied up to this time.[17]

Return to your vehicle, and continue straight about 0.2 mile to Central Avenue. Turn left (north-northeast) and drive three blocks or 0.1 mile to Third Street. Turn right (east-southeast) onto East Third Street, and continue 0.9 mile to Hawthorne Street. Turn right (south-southwest) onto Hawthorne Street, and drive one block to Fourth Street. Turn left onto Fourth Street, and drive to, and park on the right short of Orchard Knob Avenue. Leave your vehicle, and walk through the gate by the Orchard Knob Park sign. Walk to the top of Orchard Knob, and face east toward Missionary Ridge.

Stop 7—Orchard Knob

Critical Decisions: (2) Bragg Orders the Establishment of Poorly Designated Lines/Positions, (17) Grant Orders Thomas to Conduct a Demonstration, (18) Thomas's Troops Decide to Continue the Assault

Although Bragg had made Critical Decision 2, sending his soldiers to defend poorly designated lines, some two months earlier, it would now come back to haunt him. When he ordered these lines, both as an advanced skirmish line several hundred yards from the base of Missionary Ridge, and as rifle pits at the base of the ridge, Bragg was on the offense. Thus his choice was logical. However, as he turned from offensive to defensive (siege-like) operations, these lines' location became a liability. This was particularly the case for the rifle pits. While it might have been reasonable to maintain a picket line forward of the base of the ridge, Rebels on the ridge's top would have readily observed any advancing Federals. Skirmishers were used to providing early warning of enemy movements. These maneuvers would have been detected just as quickly by the aforementioned Rebel observers, sparing the killing, wounding, or capture of these pickets.

With the Confederates now on the defense, the stationing of men in rifle pits rather than entrenchments at the base of the ridge did more than expose them to death, wounding, and capture. This location also meant that the soldiers were lost while they retreated up Missionary Ridge, and that they required recovery time after that scramble. More important was the fact that these Rebels provided a screen for some Yankees. Confederates atop the ridge feared to fire down upon their own men.

Narrative of Brig. Gen. Arthur M. Manigault, CSA, Commanding Manigault's Brigade, Anderson's Division, Hardee's Corps, Army of Tennessee

The troops from below at length reached the works, exhausted and breathless, much the greater portion so demoralized, that, breaking through their friends, they rushed to the rear, bent on placing the ridge itself between them and the enemy. It required the

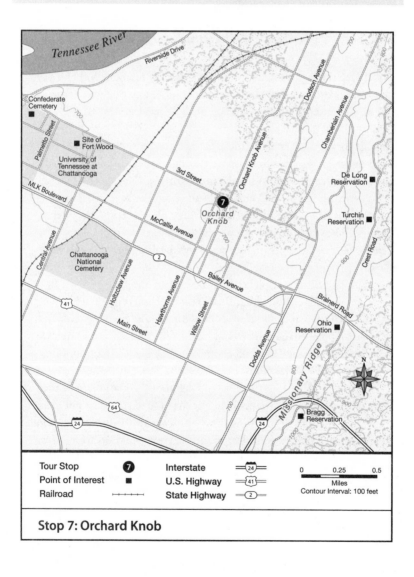

Stop 7: Orchard Knob

utmost efforts of myself, staff, and other officers, to prevent this, which we finally succeeded in doing. Many threw themselves on the ground, broken down from over-exertion, and became deathly sick, or fainted. I noticed several instances of slight hemorrhage, and it was fifteen minutes before most of these men were so recovered as to be made use of, or their nervous systems so restored as to be able to draw trigger with any steadiness.[18]

While you cannot directly see where these rifle pits and entrenchments were located, perhaps you can visualize them and follow the Confederates as they scrambled up the ridge with the Yankees in hot pursuit.

With Sherman's assault on the Confederate right flank around Tunnel Hill having ground to a halt, Grant decided to distract the enemy. Grant made Critical Decision 17 for a diversionary maneuver, ordering Thomas to make a demonstration to the base of Missionary Ridge. This Thomas did, resulting in the quick capture of the Confederate rifle pits there.

Narrative of Maj. Gen. Ulysses S. Grant, USA, Commanding Military Division of the Mississippi

But Sherman's condition was getting so critical that the assault for his relief could not be delayed any longer. . . .

Sheridan's and Wood's divisions had been lying under arms from early morning, ready to move the instant the signal was given. I now directed Thomas to order the charge at once. I watched eagerly to see the effect, and became impatient at last that there was no indication of any charge being made. The centre of the line which was to make the charge was near where Thomas and I stood, but was concealed by an intervening forest. Turning to Thomas to inquire what caused the delay, I was surprised to see Thomas J. Wood, one of the division commanders who was to make the charge, standing talking to him. I spoke to General Wood asking him why he did not charge as ordered an hour before. He replied very promptly that this was the first he had heard of it, but that he had been ready all day to move at a moment's notice. I told him to make the charge at once. He was off in a moment, and in an incredibly short time loud cheering was heard, and he and Sheridan were driving the enemy's advance before them towards Missionary Ridge.[19]

Perhaps you can visualize Thomas's four divisions before you, and to your left and right, as they advanced in perfect order toward the ridge. Realize, however, that no obstructions other than natural ones were present at that time.

Return to your vehicle. Turn right, and continue south-southwest on Orchard Knob Avenue for four blocks to the intersection with McCallie Avenue. Continue through that intersection for three more blocks to the intersection with Bailey Avenue. Turn left (east-southeast), and continue five blocks. Where the main road begins to veer left, do not follow it but continue straight ahead on Bailey Avenue a block to the intersection with Dodds Avenue. Turn right (south-southwest) onto Dodds Avenue, and continue 0.5 mile to the intersection with Main Street. Turn left (east-southeast) onto Main Street, and follow it about 0.3 mile as it winds up to the top of Missionary Ridge. On top of Missionary Ridge at the intersection with South Crest Road, turn right (south) onto South Crest Road, and immediately cross over I-24. On the south side of I-24, turn right onto South Crest Road, and follow it around 0.2 mile to the entrance to the Bragg Reservation (small park) on your left. Turn left into the Bragg Reservation, and park. Leave your vehicle, and walk to the tall Illinois Monument.

Stop 8—Bragg's Headquarters

Critical Decisions: (2) Bragg Orders the Establishment of Poorly Designated Lines/Positions, (9) Bragg Decides Longstreet Will Capture Knoxville, (12) Breckinridge Orders Captain Green to Lay Out a Topographical Crest Line of Defense, (13) Bragg Decides Cleburne Will Protect the Right Flank at Tunnel Hill, (15) Bragg Decides to Abandon Lookout Mountain

It is quite obvious from this location what an impressive defensive position Missionary Ridge offers to an army manning it. It appears virtually impregnable. Certainly, the remnants of Rosecrans's Army of the Cumberland, as they fell back from the Chickamauga battlefield, initially thought so.

Bragg's headquarters was located near here, and he made several critical decisions in this area. He assumed that the Confederate line running along the top of Missionary Ridge was simply unassailable. As noted previously, Bragg made Critical Decision 2 for his soldiers to defend a poorly designed line at the base of the ridge, with pickets posted closer to the city. While Bragg's troops were on the offensive, this appeared to be a good plan. However, when his soldiers were forced on the defensive, this strategy became unwise. As would be discovered, a Union attack would overwhelm what Rebel troops manned this line of entrenchments at the base. Defenders would be killed or captured. Even worse, they might flee back up the slope of the ridge, preventing return fire from Confederates stationed at the top.

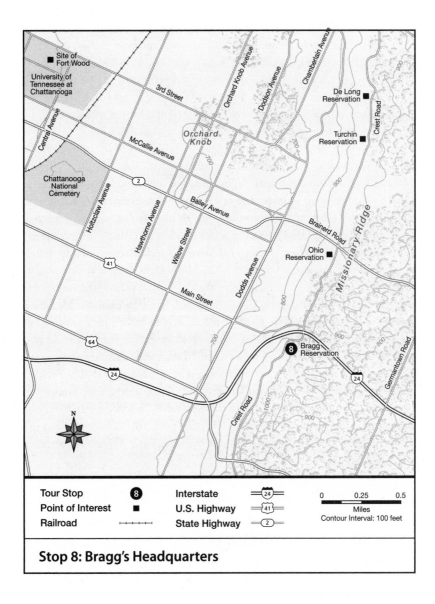

Tour Stop	⑧	Interstate		0 0.25 0.5
Point of Interest	■	U.S. Highway		Miles
Railroad		State Highway		Contour Interval: 100 feet

Stop 8: Bragg's Headquarters

Narrative of Brig. Gen. Arthur M. Manigault, CSA, Commanding Manigault's Brigade, Anderson's Division, Hardee's Corps, Army of Tennessee

The instructions given to the officers commanding the lower line were, if attacked by lines of battle, to await the approach of the enemy to within two hundred yards, deliver their fire, and then to retire to the works above, a most unwise and injudicious disposition of the forces, and the orders by which they were to be governed of a like character. Only the superior officers were made aware of the plan to be pursued, and the men were kept in ignorance of it. These two separate and distinct lines were occupied by the men in one rank, with an interval of about a pace between each soldier.[20]

Critical Decision 9, also made here, concerned Lt. Gen. James Longstreet. Longstreet had convinced both Jefferson Davis and Gen. Robert E. Lee to send his corps west to augment Bragg's Army of Tennessee. This gamble paid off with the victory at Chickamauga, but to no one's surprise, Longstreet quickly decided that Bragg was incapable of army command. Unfortunately for Longstreet, Davis saw through his finagling and firmly refused to switch commanders. Longstreet began to sulk. He hurt himself with his performance, but more importantly, he hurt the Confederacy. Longstreet's bizarre behavior when protecting the Confederate left flank on Lookout Mountain demonstrated this fact. His Critical Decision 7 to fail to protect Lookout Valley and keep the Union line of supply from stretching through it allowed for the establishment of the "Cracker Line." Longstreet blatantly disregarded Bragg's direct orders. Bragg was so alienated by this behavior that he decided Longstreet had to go, and with Critical Decision 9 Bragg sent Longstreet to relieve Knoxville. On the surface this seemed to be a good intention, one backed by Jefferson Davis. In reality, this choice further diminished Bragg's available force around Chattanooga. At the same time, Grant was working to increase his force.

Headquarters, Department of Tennessee, Missionary Ridge, November 4, 1863, General Longstreet, [CSA], Commanding Corps:

General: You will move with your command as indicated in our conference yesterday [to relieve Knoxville]. . . . Every preparation is ordered to advance you as fast as possible.[21]

Longstreet was sent away with minimum support, reducing Bragg's available force by some fifteen thousand men.[22]

Based on Thomas's reconnaissance in force that quickly captured Orchard Knob on the twenty-third, Bragg realized his center along Missionary Ridge was perhaps vulnerable to attack. He reacted with Critical Decision 15, which established a defensive line along the top of the Ridge. Logically, this order should have been given months ago. But Bragg and others believed that Missionary Ridge was simply too physical an obstacle to be overcome, and that its defenses were impregnable. Suddenly doubting himself, Bragg ordered the aforementioned defensive line. This assignment was directed to Capt. John W. Green, Maj. Gen. John C. Breckinridge's engineering officer. While Greene's exact orders are unclear, he was apparently ordered to lay the line out upon Missionary Ridge's topographical crest, not its military crest. This placement would quickly cause problems, reducing the Confederates' available fields of fire, and therefore aiding the Union troops assaulting the ridge.

Narrative of Brig. Gen. Arthur M. Manigault, CSA, Commanding Manigault's Brigade, Hindman's (Anderson's) Division, Hardee's Corps, Army of Tennessee

During the night of the 23rd, orders came to construct a line of defenses on the crest of the Missionary Ridge, and such artillery as was in position in the lines at the foot was brought away. . . . This new line was run out by an engineer officer, whose name I have forgotten. He appeared to be in a great hurry, and said that he had much to do. Not liking the line that he proposed laying out for me, I suggested that if he would leave it to me, I would relieve him of the trouble, and as I was to be responsible for the defense of a certain amount of front, it might reasonably be expected that I would lay it out to the greatest advantage. This he agreed to do, and seemed much pleased at being relieved of some portion of his work, but at the same time told me that his instructions were to run the line on the highest point or outline of the hill. This was just what I wanted to avoid doing, for by doing so, I noticed that at many points, an intervening projection or irregularity of the downward slope prevented the fire of the defenders from playing on the enemy, after their reaching the foot of the ridge and when they ascended. The same obstacle protected them until within 15, 20, or 30 yards of our works. The only way in which this difficulty could be obviated was by selecting the ground when such was the case, below the crest, but whenever it was practicable and could be done, to make use of the highest ground. This defect I noticed in the line of the other brigades, and called attention to it, but it was not deemed worthy of notice, and we paid dearly for it on the day after.[23]

Here Bragg made Critical Decision 13, dispatching Maj. Gen. Patrick Cleburne to protect the Confederate right flank at Tunnel Hill. Although slow to perceive Grant's intentions, Bragg had finally deduced that the Union general's plan of attack was to roll up the Rebels' largely unprotected right flank.

In another unwise, quickly rescinded decision, Bragg had decided to send more troops off to augment Longstreet and recapture Knoxville. He did so at the expense of further reducing his forces manning the supposed siege line around Chattanooga. The demonstration that Grant ordered and Maj. Gen. George H. Thomas's Army of the Cumberland executed to capture Orchard Knob caught Bragg unawares. Ascertaining that Grant was now on the offensive, Bragg recalled what troops he was able to Chattanooga. Further realizing the vulnerability of his right flank, Bragg sought to immediately protect it. He called upon Cleburne, perhaps his finest division commander, to undertake this assignment. In fact, Cleburne's positioning at Tunnel Hill saved Bragg's army from sooner defeat. Cleburne's stand there was a magnificent demonstration of tactical brilliance.

Report of Maj. Gen. Patrick Cleburne, CSA, Commanding Cleburne's Division, Breckinridge's Corps, Army of Tennessee

I had sent off all of Buckner's division except Reynolds [*sic*] brigade when I received the following order[s] from army headquarters, viz:

The general commanding desires that you will halt such portions of your command as have not yet left at Chickamauga [station]. . . . Move up rapidly with your whole force. . . . We are heavily engaged. Move rapidly to these headquarters.[24]

Critical Decision 15, Bragg's final one here, was to abandon Lookout Mountain. Less concerned with the value of holding Lookout Mountain, and increasingly concerned about protecting his right flank at Tunnel Hill, Bragg ordered his troops to withdraw from the mountain on November 24. Those soldiers who had defended it would instead augment his center and right flank. Bragg had realized he was trying to protect too wide of an area from an enemy continually increasing its numbers available for combat. After hearing of requests for more reinforcements for Lookout Mountain—of which he had none to spare—Bragg's orders were as follows (as seen at Stop 3):

> ### Headquarters, Army of Tennessee, November 24, 2:30 p.m., Maj. Gen. C. L. Stevenson, [CSA], Lookout Mountain
>
> General: The general commanding instructs me to say that you will withdraw your command from the mountain to this side [east] of Chickamauga Creek, destroying the bridges behind. Fight the enemy as you retire. The thickness of the fog will enable you to retire, it is hoped, without much difficulty.[25]

Return to your vehicle. Turn right (northwest) out of the Bragg Reservation onto South Crest Road, retracing your drive 0.2 mile back to a left turn (north) onto South Crest Road. Continue north on South Crest Road across the bridge over I-24. Continue north 0.9 mile until reaching the intersection with Birds Mill Road. Here South Crest Road becomes North Crest Road. Remain on North Crest Road, and continue 0.4 mile to the De Long Reservation (small park) on your left. Park, leave your vehicle, and walk to the tall monument dedicated to the Second Minnesota Infantry. Face Chattanooga and visualize the Union advancing toward you. Move carefully to a place where you can look down at the steep slope the Yankee soldiers had to climb.

Stop 9—De Long Reservation, Union Breakthrough/Confederate Collapse

Critical Decisions: (12) Breckinridge Orders Captain Green to Lay Out a Topographical Crest Line of Defense, (17) Grant Orders Thomas to Conduct a Demonstration, (18) Union Troops Decide to Continue the Assault

This stop gives a sense of the terrain the men of Thomas's army had to scale—obviously a serious obstacle. Had this area been properly manned by well-entrenched Rebels, it is hard to believe that any assault would have succeeded.

Turn around, and look back at the top of Missionary Ridge.

At and near this position, the Crest Road somewhat approximates the military crest (see the information and diagram below). The homes are situated on the topographical crest; note how much higher it is. Further note how

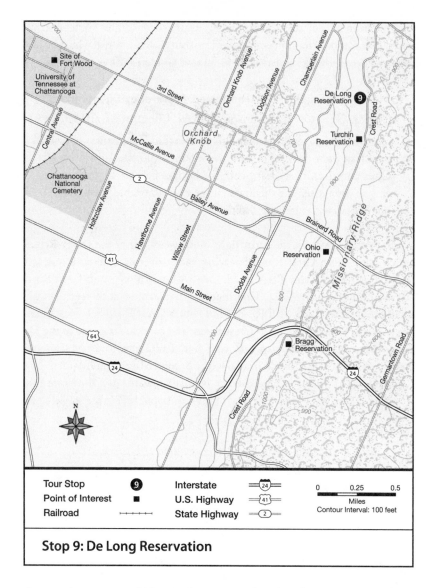

Legend:

Tour Stop	**9**	Interstate	24
Point of Interest	■	U.S. Highway	41
Railroad	+—+—+	State Highway	2

0 — 0.25 — 0.5
Miles
Contour Interval: 100 feet

Stop 9: De Long Reservation

depressed cannon would have to be to cover the area where you are standing. After scaling the ridge to just below the Second Minnesota Monument's location, the Yankees would have found a brief sanctuary in which to regroup before making their final assault on the Rebel line.

Military crest is a term in military science referring to "an area on the forward or reverse slope of a hill or ridge just below the topographical crest from which maximum observation and direct fire covering the slope down to the base of the hill or ridge can be obtained."[26]

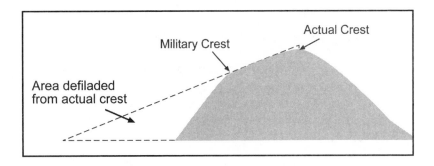

Troops maneuvering along the side of a hill or ridge use the military crest to obtain maximum visibility of the terrain below and minimize their own visibility. At the actual or topographical crest of the hill, soldiers would be silhouetted against the sky. This was not the case at the military crest.[27]

Observation points (OPs) can be located at the military crest if the main defensive position is located on the reverse slope of the hill or ridge. This is usually the case when a main defensive position at the military crest would be vulnerable to the enemy's artillery, making coordinated withdrawal difficult.[28]

The main defensive position can be located at the military crest if it is secure against a strong attack. Defending troops would then have the best ability to not only see the attacking forces but also bring maximum firepower to bear at the earliest opportunity.[29]

As Sherman did not appear to be making headway on Bragg's right flank, Grant considered a diversionary maneuver appropriate. With Critical Decision 17 he ordered Thomas to make a demonstration by advancing to and capturing the rifle pits at the base of Missionary Ridge, just below you. Thomas successfully obeyed this order.

Narrative of Peter Cozzens, Describing
Maj. Gen. Ulysses S. Grant, USA, on Orchard Knob

"General Sherman seems to be having a hard time," Grant said absently. Yes General, he does seem to be in a warm place," answered [Brig. Gen. Thomas J.] Wood, not quite sure how to respond to Grant's statement of the obvious.

Grant was groping for a solution: "It does seem as if he is having a hard time, and it seems as if we ought to help him."

Wood, followed the tentative flow of Grant's thinking. "I think so too, General, and whatever you order we will try to do," he said.

Wood's gentle nudge helped Grant make up his mind. "If you and Sheridan advance your divisions to the foot of the ridge, and there halt, I think it will menace Bragg's forces so as to relieve Sherman," Grant speculated.

"Perhaps it might work in that way, and if you order it, we will try it, and I think we can carry the intrenchments [*sic*] at the base of the ridge," answered Wood.[30]

As is now well-known, Thomas's men found themselves in a virtually untenable position after capturing the Confederate rifle pits at the base of Missionary Ridge. Remaining at the base would allow them to be picked off by the Rebels above. As a result, Thomas's men began to climb the slope of Missionary Ridge. It is not clear who ordered this action: it seemed to be a commonsense solution. Critical Decision 18 to continue the assault up the slope resulted in victory for the Union. This was likely a collective decision reached by soldiers at all levels of command. Initially Grant was displeased, but he quickly changed his mind as Thomas's soldiers began their ascent.

Report of Brig. Gen. August Willich, USA, Commanding First Brigade, Third Division, Fourth Army Corps, Army of the Cumberland

On the given signal the brigade advanced in quick time, but shell and spherical case fell very thick, and all the regiments double-quicked until they reached the rebel rifle-pits and camps at the foot of the ridge, driving the enemy's infantry before them, all his artillery being on the crest of the ridge. It was evident to every one [*sic*] that to stay in this position would be certain destruction and final defeat; every soldier felt the necessity of saving the day and the campaign by conquering, and every one saw instinctively that the only place of safety was in the enemy's works on the crest of the ridge.[31]

Return to your vehicle. Continue north on North Crest Road for 2.0 miles to the intersection with Lightfoot Mill Road to the right (northeast). Turn right (northeast) onto the Lightfoot Mill Road, and look for the sign identifying Sherman Reservation. Park in the designated area on the right shoulder, opposite the footpath by the artillery display leading (north) into the Sherman Reservation (or park). Walk along the footpath some three hundred yards (uphill) to the tall Iowa Monument. Face northeast.

Stop 10—*Cleburne's Defense of the Right Flank*

Critical Decisions: (10) Grant Orders Sherman to Attack Bragg's Right at Tunnel Hill, (13) Bragg Decides That Cleburne Will Protect the Right Flank at Tunnel Hill, (14) Sherman Decides to Entrench and Not Attack Tunnel Hill (16) Sherman Decides to Attack with Two of Nine Brigades

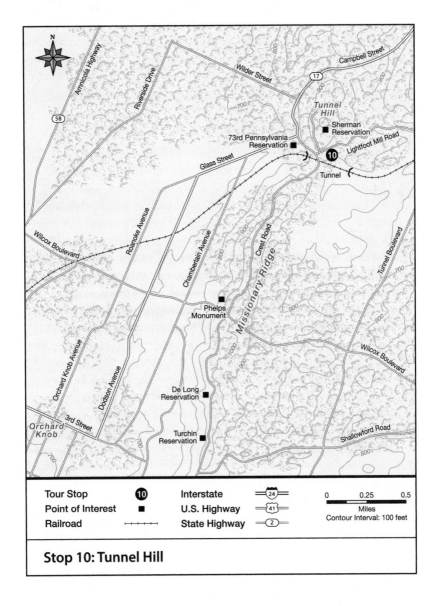

Stop 10: Tunnel Hill

Grant was impatient for the arrival of the troops marching to his relief. While awaiting them, he formulated a plan of attack he would implement once all his reinforcements were in place. Grant's Critical Decision 10 assigned the main assault to his good and trusted friend Maj. Gen. William T. Sherman. This offensive would take place on the north end of Missionary Ridge, where Sherman would attempt to roll up the Rebel right flank. This task would be his focus in attempting to break out of Chattanooga, and escape from the city would depend on his success. All other offensive actions would be conducted relative to Sherman's main assault. In Grant's opinion, the Rebel right flank did not appear strong and/or well defended. After Sherman had crossed the Tennessee River early on November 24, he had cautiously advanced to the north end of Missionary Ridge (Lightburn Hill).

Narrative of Maj. Gen. William T. Sherman, USA, Commanding Army of the Tennessee

About midnight I received, at the hands of Major Rowley, of General Grant's staff, orders to attack the enemy at dawn of day, and notice that General Thomas would attack in force early in the day. Accordingly, before day, I was in the saddle, attended by all my staff; rode to the extreme left of our position, near Chickamauga; thence up the hill held by General Lightburn, and round to the extreme right of General Ewing, catching as accurate an idea of the ground as possible by the dim light of morning. I saw that our line of attack was in the direction of Missionary Ridge, with wings supporting on either flank.

Quite a valley lay between us and the next hill of the series, and this hill presented steep sides, the one to the west partially cleared, but the other covered with the native forest. The crest of the ridge was narrow and wooded. The farther point of the hill was held by the enemy with a breastwork of logs and fresh earth, filled with men and two guns. The enemy was also seen in great force on a still higher hill beyond the tunnel, from which he had a fair plunging fire on the hill in dispute.[32]

Bragg made Critical Decision 13 to recall Cleburne from his originally assigned movement to Knoxville. When he reported to Bragg at his headquarters, Cleburne was ordered to protect the Confederate right flank at Tunnel Hill. He responded just in time, successfully defending the right flank until the Rebel line was broken to his left on Missionary Ridge. At this point, Cleburne was directed to retreat.

Report of Maj. Gen. Patrick R. Cleburne, CSA, Commanding Cleburne's Division, Breckinridge's Corps, Army of Tennessee

About 2 p.m. on 24th November, I received orders to proceed with the remaining three brigades of my division to the right of Missionary Ridge, near the point where the tunnel of the East Tennessee and Georgia Railroad passes through Missionary Ridge, where I would find an officer of General Hardee's staff, who would show me my position. Bragg informed me that the enemy had already a division in line opposite the position I was intended to occupy; that he was rapidly crossing another, and had nearly completed a pontoon bridge over the Tennessee opposite my position. He also told me I must preserve the railroad bridge in my rear, where Brigadier-General Polk was stationed, at all hazards.[33]

Sherman simply was not having a good day on November 24. Faced with the discovery that he was not, in fact, on Tunnel Hill but separated from it by a large chasm, he made Critical Decision 14 to stop his forward movement and entrench. This choice ended his advance for the day, allowing Cleburne additional time to fortify his position on Tunnel Hill.

Early on the morning of the twenty-fifth, Sherman, obeying Grant's order noted above, ordered an attack against Cleburne's well-entrenched position atop Tunnel Hill. However, rather than ordering an all-out assault by at least parts of his four available divisions, Sherman made Critical Decision 16 to send in only a couple of brigades. These troops would attack the narrow front available to him. Had he utilized more of his available troops, Sherman could potentially have bypassed Cleburne's position on either or both flanks.

Return to your vehicle. Leave the parking area, and return to North Crest Road. Turn left (south) onto North Crest Road, and drive south 2.4 miles to the intersection with Birds Mill Avenue. Here North Crest Drive changes name to South Crest Drive. Continue south on South Crest Drive for 1.0 mile, crossing over I-24. Turn right (west) onto and continue to follow South Crest Road south 3.0 miles (2.8 miles from the Bragg Reservation) to the intersection on the left (east) with John Ross Road. Carefully turn sharply left onto John Ross Road, and follow it generally east 1.6 miles to the intersection with US 41/Ringgold Highway. Turn right (east) onto US

Highway 41, and continue 10.6 miles, (passing under I-75 at 2.6 miles) to the intersection with Georgia Highway 151 in downtown Ringgold. You will be following the general line of retreat of the Confederate army. As you enter Ringgold, US Highway 41 is also labeled Nashville Street. Nashville Street intersects the Alabama Highway or Georgia Highway 151 at a stoplight in downtown. Continue east on Nashville Street 0.9 mile to just before the railroad overpass. Turn left into the parking lot at the old Ringgold Depot. Park here, leave your vehicle, walk to the pedestrian bridge crossing over US 41, and face east, looking at the gap in front of you.

Stop 11—Cleburne's Rear Guard Defense at Ringgold

Critical Decision 19: Bragg Orders Cleburne to Protect the Confederate Retreat

To prevent further disaster, Gen. Braxton Bragg knew he had to assign a rear guard to protect his men as they continued retreating south to Dalton. In front of you is Ringgold Gap. It was an excellent defensive position, and Bragg hoped it could be secured at least long enough to allow his men to safely evacuate. Therefore he made Critical Decision 19, the final one of the Chattanooga Campaign, to assign Maj. Gen. Patrick R. Cleburne to command the army's rear guard, consisting of his division. The fate of Bragg's army rested on Cleburne's shoulders. Bragg knew that Cleburne was the best division commander in his army, and that he and his division were the most likely to hold off the pursuing Yankees.

Report of Maj. Gen. Patrick R. Cleburne, CSA, Commanding Cleburne's Division, Breckinridge's Corps, Army of Tennessee

At 3 a.m. on the 27th, I received the following order, viz:
Major-General Cleburne:

General: The general desires that you will take strong position in the gorge of the mountain [Ringgold Gap] and attempt to check pursuit of enemy. He must be punished until our trains and the rear of our troops get well advanced. The reports from the rear are meager and the general is not thoroughly advised of the state of things there. Will you be good enough to report fully?

Respectfully,
George W M Brent
Assistant Adjutant-general[34]

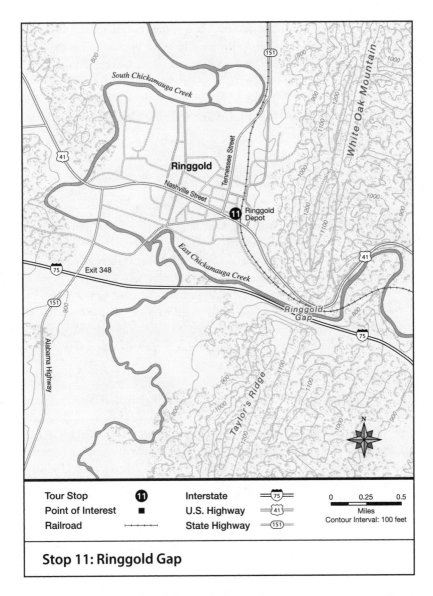

Tour Stop ⑪ **Interstate** 〔75〕
Point of Interest ■ **U.S. Highway** 〔41〕
Railroad ├─┼─┼─┤ **State Highway** 〔151〕

0   0.25   0.5
Miles
Contour Interval: 100 feet

Stop 11: Ringgold Gap

On November 27 Cleburne held off Union attacks all morning and into the early afternoon. He was then advised that Bragg's army was safely away toward Dalton. Cleburne subsequently placed his men along the ridges in front of you and carefully hid some artillery at the gap.

A less motived or less reliable division commander than Cleburne might have faltered in leading the rear guard. Had Union pursuit been successful, Bragg's already-defeated army could have suffered many more casualties and perhaps even virtual disbandment. As it turned out, Cleburne held off a foe three times larger than his division while losing only 20 of his men and suffering a total of 221 casualties. It was truly a magnificent action at Ringgold Gap.[35]

Joint Resolution of the Confederate Congress

No. 16. JOINT RESOLUTION of thanks to Maj. Gen. Patrick R. Cleburne, and the officers and men under his command, for distinguished service at Ringgold Gap, in the State of Georgia November 27, 1863,

Resolved, That the thanks of Congress are due, and are hereby tendered, to Maj. Gen. Patrick R. Cleburne and the officers and men under his command, for the victory obtained by them over superior forces of the enemy at Ringgold Ga, in the State of Georgia, on the 27th day of November, 1863, by which the advance

of the enemy was impeded, our wagon train and most of our artillery saved, and a large number of the enemy killed and wounded.

Resolved, That the President be requested to communicate the foregoing resolution to Major-General Cleburne and his command.

Approved, February 9, 1864.[36]

This concludes the tour of some of the sites where critical decisions were made before and during the Battle of Chattanooga. If desired, you may continue generally south on US Highway 41 to Dalton. For easy access to I-75 in either direction, return to downtown Ringgold to the intersection with the Alabama Highway, Georgia Highway 151. Turn left (south) onto Highway 151, and continue 0.4 mile to the entrance ramps to I-75.

APPENDIX II

UNION ORDER OF BATTLE

MILITARY DIVISION OF THE MISSISSIPPI
Maj. Gen. Ulysses S. Grant

ARMY OF THE CUMBERLAND
Maj. Gen. George H. Thomas

GENERAL HEADQUARTERS
1st Ohio Sharpshooters
10th Ohio Infantry

FOURTH ARMY CORPS
Maj. Gen. Gordon Granger

FIRST DIVISION
Brig. Gen. Charles Cruft
ESCORT
92nd Illinois, Company B
FIRST BRIGADE
Guarding lines of supply

SECOND BRIGADE
Brig. Gen. Walter C. Whitaker
96th Illinois
35th Indiana

8th Kentucky
40th Ohio
51st Ohio
99th Ohio

THIRD BRIGADE
Col. William Grose
59th Illinois
75th Illinois
84th Illinois
9th Indiana
36th Indiana
24th Ohio

SECOND DIVISION
Maj. Gen. Philip H. Sheridan

FIRST BRIGADE
Col. Francis T. Sherman
36th Illinois
44th Illinois
73rd Illinois
74th Illinois
88th Illinois
22nd Indiana
2nd Missouri
15th Missouri
24th Wisconsin

SECOND BRIGADE
Brig. Gen. George D. Wagner
100th Illinois
15th Indiana
40th Indiana
51st Indiana
57th Indiana
58th Indiana
26th Ohio
97th Ohio

THIRD BRIGADE
Col. Charles G. Harker
22nd Illinois
27th Illinois

42nd Illinois
51st Illinois
79th Illinois
3rd Kentucky
64th Ohio
65th Ohio
125th Ohio

ARTILLERY
Capt. Warren P. Edgarton
1st Illinois Light, Battery M
10th Indiana Battery
1st Missouri Light, Battery G
1st Ohio Light, Battery I
4th United States, Battery G
5th United States, Battery H

THIRD DIVISION
Brig. Gen. Thomas J. Wood

FIRST BRIGADE
Brig. Gen. August Willich
25th Illinois
35th Illinois
89th Illinois
32nd Indiana
68th Indiana
8th Kansas
15th Ohio
49th Ohio
15th Wisconsin

SECOND BRIGADE
Brig. Gen. William B. Hazen
6th Indiana
5th Kentucky
6th Kentucky
23rd Kentucky
1st Ohio
6th Ohio
41st Ohio
93rd Ohio
124th Ohio

THIRD BRIGADE
  Brig. Gen. Samuel Beatty
  79th Indiana
  86th Indiana
  9th Kentucky
  17th Kentucky
  13th Ohio
  19th Ohio
  59th Ohio

ARTILLERY
  Capt. Cullen Bradley
  Illinois Light, Bridge's Battery
  6th Ohio Battery
  20th Ohio Battery
  Pennsylvania Light, Battery B

ELEVENTH ARMY CORPS
  Maj. Gen. Oliver O. Howard

GENERAL HEADQUARTERS
  Independent Company, 8th New York

SECOND DIVISION
  Brig. Gen. Adolph von Steinwehr

FIRST BRIGADE
  Col. Adolphus Bushbeck
  33rd New Jersey
  134th New York
  154th New York
  27th Pennsylvania
  73rd Pennsylvania

SECOND BRIGADE
  Col. Orland Smith
  33rd Massachusetts
  136th New York
  55th Ohio
  73rd Ohio

THIRD DIVISION
   Maj. Gen. Carl Schurz
FIRST BRIGADE
   Brig. Gen. Hector Tyndale
   101st Illinois
   45th New York
   143rd New York
   61st Ohio
   82nd Ohio

SECOND BRIGADE
   Col. Wladimir Krzyzanowski
   58th New York
   119th New York
   141st New York
   26th Wisconsin

THIRD BRIGADE
   Col. Frederick Hecker
   80th Illinois
   82nd Illinois
   68th New York
   75th Pennsylvania

ARTILLERY
   Maj. Thomas W. Osborn
   1st New York Light, Battery I
   New York Light, 13th Battery
   1st Ohio Light, Battery I
   1st Ohio Light, Battery K
   4th United States, Battery G

TWELFTH ARMY CORPS
   Maj. Gen. Henry W. Slocum

FIRST DIVISION
   Guarding railroad
SECOND DIVISION
   Brig. Gen. John W. Geary
FIRST BRIGADE
   Col. Charles Candy
   Col. William R. Creighton

Col. Thomas J. Ahl
5th Ohio
7th Ohio
29th Ohio
66th Ohio
28th Pennsylvania
147th Pennsylvania

SECOND BRIGADE
Col. George A. Cobham Jr.
29th Pennsylvania
109th Pennsylvania
111th Pennsylvania

THIRD BRIGADE
Maj. Gen. George S. Greene
Col. David Ireland
60th New York
78th New York
102nd New York
137th New York
149th New York

ARTILLERY
Maj. John A. Reynolds
Pennsylvania Light, Battery E
5th United States, Battery K

FOURTEENTH CORPS
Maj. Gen. John M. Palmer

ESCORT
1st Ohio Cavalry

FIRST DIVISION
Brig. Gen. Richard W. Johnson

FIRST BRIGADE
Brig. Gen. William P. Carlin
104th Illinois
38th Indiana
42nd Indiana
88th Indiana
2nd Ohio

33rd Ohio
94th Ohio
10th Wisconsin

SECOND BRIGADE
    Col. Marshall F. Moore
    Col. William L. Stoughton
    19th Illinois
    11th Michigan
    69th Ohio
    15th United States, 1st and 2nd Battalions
    16th United States, 1st Battalion
    18th United States, 1st and 2nd Battalions
    19th United States, 1st Battalion

THIRD BRIGADE
    Brig. Gen. John C. Starkweather
    24th Illinois
    37th Indiana
    21st Ohio
    74th Ohio
    78th Pennsylvania
    79th Pennsylvania
    1st Wisconsin
    21st Wisconsin

ARTILLERY
    1st Illinois Light, Battery C
    1st Michigan Light, Battery A
    5th United States, Battery H

SECOND DIVISION
    Brig. Gen. Jefferson C. Davis

FIRST BRIGADE
    Brig. Gen. James D. Morgan
    10th Illinois
    16th Illinois
    60th Illinois
    21st Kentucky
    10th Michigan
    14th Michigan

SECOND BRIGADE
  Brig. Gen. John Beatty
  34th Illinois
  78th Illinois
  3rd Ohio
  98th Ohio
  108th Ohio
  113th Ohio
  121st Ohio

THIRD BRIGADE
  Col. Daniel McCook
  85th Illinois
  86th Illinois
  110th Illinois
  125th Illinois
  52nd Ohio

ARTILLERY
  Capt. William A. Hotchkiss
  2nd Illinois Light, Battery I
  Minnesota Light, 2nd Battery
  Wisconsin Light, 5th Battery

THIRD DIVISION
  Brig. Gen. Absalom Baird

FIRST BRIGADE
  Brig. Gen. John B. Turchin
  82nd Indiana
  11th Ohio
  17th Ohio
  31st Ohio
  36th Ohio
  89th Ohio
  92nd Ohio

SECOND BRIGADE
  Col. Ferdinand Van Derveer
  75th Indiana
  87th Indiana
  101st Indiana
  2nd Minnesota

9th Ohio
35th Ohio
105th Ohio

THIRD BRIGADE
Col. Edward H. Phelps
Col. William H. Hays
10th Indiana
74th Indiana
4th Kentucky
10th Kentucky
18th Kentucky
14th Ohio
38th Ohio

ARTILLERY
Capt. George R. Swallow
Indiana Light, 7th Battery
Indiana Light, 19th Battery
4th United States, Battery I

ENGINEER TROOPS
Brig. Gen. William F. Smith

ENGINEERS
1st Michigan Engineers (detachment)
13th Michigan Infantry
21st Michigan Infantry
22nd Michigan Infantry
18th Ohio Infantry

PIONEER BRIGADE
Col. George P. Buell
1st Battalion
2nd Battalion
3rd Battalion

ARTILLERY RESERVE
Brig. Gen. John M. Brannan

FIRST DIVISION
Col. James Barnett

FIRST BRIGADE
 Maj. Charles S. Cotter
 1st Ohio Light, Battery B
 1st Ohio Light, Battery C
 1st Ohio Light, Battery E
 1st Ohio Light, Battery F

SECOND BRIGADE
 1st Ohio Light, Battery G
 1st Ohio Light, Battery M
 Ohio Light, 18th Battery
 Ohio Light, 20th Battery

SECOND DIVISION

FIRST BRIGADE
 Capt. Josiah W. Church
 1st Michigan Light, Battery D
 1st Tennessee Light, Battery A
 Wisconsin Light, 3rd Battery
 Wisconsin Light, 8th Battery
 Wisconsin Light, 10th Battery

SECOND BRIGADE
 Capt. Arnold Sutermeister
 Indiana Light, 4th Battery
 Indiana Light, 8th Battery
 Indiana Light, 11th Battery
 Indiana Light, 21st Battery
 1st Wisconsin Heavy, Company C

CAVALRY

SECOND BRIGADE (SECOND DIVISION)
 Col. Eli Long
 98th Illinois (Mounted Infantry)
 17th Indiana (Mounted Infantry)
 2nd Kentucky
 4th Michigan
 1st Ohio
 3rd Ohio
 4th Ohio
 10th Ohio

POST OF CHATTANOOGA
Col. John G. Parkhurst
44th Indiana
15th Kentucky
9th Michigan

ARMY OF THE TENNESSEE
Maj. Gen. William T. Sherman

FIFTEENTH ARMY CORPS

FIRST DIVISION
Brig. Gen. Peter J. Osterhaus

FIRST BRIGADE
Brig. Gen. Charles R. Woods
13th Illinois
3rd Missouri
12th Missouri
17th Missouri
27th Missouri
29th Missouri
31st Missouri
32nd Missouri
76th Ohio

SECOND BRIGADE
Col. James A. Williamson
4th Iowa
9th Iowa
25th Iowa
26th Iowa
30th Iowa
31st Iowa

ARTILLERY
Capt. Henry H. Griffiths
Iowa Light, 1st Battery
2nd Missouri Light, Battery F
Ohio Light, 4th Battery

SECOND DIVISION
Brig. Gen. Morgan L. Smith

FIRST BRIGADE
    Brig. Gen. Giles A. Smith
    Col. Nathan W. Tupper
    55th Illinois
    116th Illinois
    127th Illinois
    6th Missouri
    8th Missouri
    57th Ohio
    13th United States, 1st Battalion

SECOND BRIGADE
    Brig. Gen. Joseph A. J. Lightburn
    83rd Indiana
    30th Ohio
    37th Ohio
    47th Ohio
    54th Ohio
    4th West Virginia

ARTILLERY
    1st Illinois Light, Battery A
    1st Illinois Light, Battery B
    1st Illinois Light, Battery H

THIRD DIVISION
    Brig. Gen. James M. Tuttle
    At Memphis, La Grange, and Pocahontas, Tennessee

FOURTH DIVISION
    Brig. Gen Hugh Ewing

FIRST BRIGADE
    Col. John M. Loomis
    26th Illinois
    90th Illinois
    12th Indiana
    100th Indiana

SECOND BRIGADE
>
> Brig. Gen. John M. Corse
> Col. Charles C. Walcutt
> 40th Illinois
> 103rd Illinois
> 6th Iowa
> 15th Michigan
> 46th Ohio

THIRD BRIGADE
>
> Col. Joseph R. Cockerill
> 48th Illinois
> 97th Indiana
> 99th Indiana
> 53rd Ohio
> 70th Ohio

ARTILLERY
>
> Capt. Henry Richardson
> 1st Illinois Light, Battery F
> 1st Illinois Light, Battery I
> 1st Missouri Light, Battery D

SEVENTEENTH ARMY CORPS

SECOND DIVISION
>
> Brig. Gen. John E. Smith

FIRST BRIGADE
>
> Col. Jessie I. Alexander
> 63rd Illinois
> 48th Indiana
> 59th Indiana
> 4th Minnesota
> 18th Wisconsin

SECOND BRIGADE
>
> Col. Green B. Raum
> Col. Clark R. Wever
> Col. Francis C. Deimling
> 56th Illinois
> 17th Iowa

10th Missouri
24th Missouri
80th Ohio

THIRD BRIGADE
Brig. Gen. Charles L. Matthies
Col. Benjamin D. Dean
Col. Jabez Banbury
93rd Illinois
5th Iowa
10th Iowa
26th Missouri

ARTILLERY
Capt. Henry Dillon
Cogswell's (Illinois) Battery
Wisconsin Light, 6th Battery
Wisconsin Light, 12th Battery

APPENDIX III

CONFEDERATE ORDER OF BATTLE

ARMY OF TENNESSEE
Gen. Braxton Bragg

GENERAL HEADQUARTERS
1st Louisiana (Regulars)
1st Louisiana Cavalry

LONGSTREET'S ARMY CORPS
Lieut. Gen. James Longstreet

McCLAWS'S DIVISION
Maj. Gen. Lafayette McLaws

KERSHAW'S BRIGADE
Brig. Gen. Joseph B. Kershaw
2nd South Carolina
3rd South Carolina
7th South Carolina
8th South Carolina
15th South Carolina
3rd South Carolina Battalion

HUMPHREYS'S BRIGADE
Brig. Gen. Benjamin G. Humphreys
13th Mississippi
17th Mississippi
18th Mississippi
21st Mississippi

WOFFORD'S BRIGADE
Brig. Gen. William Wofford
16th Georgia
18th Georgia
24th Georgia
Cobb's Legion
Phillips's Legion
3rd Georgia Battalion Sharpshooters

BRYAN'S BRIGADE
Brig. Gen. Goode Bryan
10th Georgia
50th Georgia
51st Georgia
53rd Georgia

ARTILLERY BATTALION
Maj. Austin Leyden
Battery C, 9th Georgia Artillery Battalion, Capt. Andrew M. Wolihin
Battery D, 9th Georgia Artillery Battalion, Capt. Tyler M. Peeples
Battery E, 9th Georgia Artillery Battalion, Capt. Billington W. York

HOOD'S DIVISION
Brig. Gen. Micah Jenkins

JENKINS'S BRIGADE
Col. John Bratton
1st South Carolina
2nd South Carolina Rifles
5th South Carolina
6th South Carolina
Hampton (South Carolina) Legion
Palmetto (South Carolina) Sharpshooters

ROBERTSON'S BRIGADE
Brig. Gen. Jerome B. Robertson
3rd Arkansas

1st Texas
4th Texas
5th Texas

LAW'S BRIGADE
Brig. Gen. E. McIver Law
4th Alabama
15th Alabama
44th Alabama
47th Alabama
48th Alabama

ANDERSON'S BRIGADE
Brig. Gen. George Anderson
7th Georgia
8th Georgia
9th Georgia
11th Georgia
59th Georgia

BENNING'S BRIGADE
Brig. Gen. Henry L. Benning
2nd Georgia
15th Georgia
17th Georgia
20th Georgia

ARTILLERY BATTALION
Col. E. Porter Alexander
Madison Louisiana Battery, Capt. George V. Moody
Brooks South Carolina Battery, Capt. William W. Fickling
Bedford Virginia Battery, Capt. Tyler C. Jordan
Parker's Virginia Battery, Capt. William W. Parker
Taylor's Virginia Battery, Capt. Osmond B. Taylor
Ashland Virginia Artillery, Capt. Pichegru Woolfolk Jr.

HARDEE'S ARMY CORPS
Lieut. Gen. William J. Hardee

CHEATHAM'S DIVISION
Brig. Gen. John K. Jackson
Maj. Gen. Benjamin F. Cheatham

JACKSON'S BRIGADE
  Brig. Gen. John K. Jackson
  1st Georgia (Confederate)
  5th Georgia
  47th Georgia
  65th Georgia
  2nd Georgia Battalion Sharpshooters
  5th Mississippi
  8th Mississippi

MOORE'S BRIGADE
  Brig. Gen. John C. Moore
  37th Alabama
  40th Alabama
  42nd Alabama

WALTHALL'S BRIGADE
  Brig. Gen. Edward C. Walthall
  24th/27th Mississippi
  29th/30th Mississippi
  34th Mississippi

WRIGHT'S BRIGADE
  Brig. Gen. Marcus J. Wright
  8th Tennessee
  16th Tennessee
  28th Tennessee
  38th Tennessee
  51st/52nd Tennessee
  Murray's (Tennessee) Battalion

ARTILLERY BATTALION
  Maj. Melancthon Smith
  Fowler's Alabama Battery, Capt. William H. Fowler
  Marion Florida Artillery, Capt. Robert P. McCants
  Griffin Georgia Light Artillery Battery, Capt. John Scogin
  Smith's Mississippi Battery, Lieut.. William B. Turner

HINDMAN'S DIVISION
  Brig. Gen. Patton Anderson

ANDERSON'S BRIGADE
  Col. William F. Tucker
  7th Mississippi

9th Mississippi
10th Mississippi
41st Mississippi
44th Mississippi
9th Mississippi Battalion Sharpshooters

MANIGAULT'S BRIGADE
Brig. Gen. Arthur M. Manigault
24th Alabama
28th Alabama
34th Alabama
10th/19th South Carolina

DEAS'S BRIGADE
Brig. Gen. Zachariah Deas
19th Alabama
22nd Alabama
25th Alabama
39th Alabama
50th Alabama
17th Alabama Battalion Sharpshooters

VAUGHAN'S BRIGADE
Brig. Gen. Alfred J. Vaughan Jr.
11th Tennessee
12th/47th Tennessee
13th/154th Tennessee
29th Tennessee

ARTILLERY BATTALION
Maj. Alfred R. Courtney
Dent's Alabama Battery, Capt. S. H. Dent
Garrity's Alabama Battery, Capt. James Garrity
Water's Alabama Battery, Lieut.. William P. Hamilton
Scott's Tennessee Battery, Capt. John Doscher

BUCKNER'S DIVISION
Brig. Gen. Bushrod R. Johnson

JOHNSON'S BRIGADE
Col. John S. Fulton
17th/23rd Tennessee
25th/44th Tennessee
63rd Tennessee

GRACIE'S BRIGADE
Brig. Gen. Archibald Gracie Jr.
41st Alabama
43rd Alabama
1st Battalion, Alabama (Hilliard's) Legion
2nd Battalion, Alabama (Hilliard's) Legion
3rd Battalion, Alabama (Hilliard's) Legion
4th Battalion, Alabama (Hilliard's) Legion

REYNOLDS'S BRIGADE
Brig. Gen. Alexander W. Reynolds
58th North Carolina
60th North Carolina
54th Virginia
63rd Virginia

ARTILLERY BATTALION
Maj. Samuel C. Williams
Barbour Alabama Artillery, Capt. R. F. Kolb
Jefferson Mississippi Artillery, Lieut. H. W. Bullen
Nottoway Virginia Artillery, Capt. William C. Jeffress

WALKER'S DIVISION
Brig. Gen. States Rights Gist

MANEY'S BRIGADE
Brig. Gen. George E. Maney
1st/27th Tennessee
4th Tennessee (Provisional Army)
6th/9th Tennessee
41st Tennessee
50th Tennessee
24th Tennessee Battalion Sharpshooters

GIST'S BRIGADE
Col. James McCullough
48th Georgia
8th Georgia Battalion
16th South Carolina
24th South Carolina

WILSON'S BRIGADE
Brig. Gen. Claudius C. Wilson
25th Georgia

29th Georgia
30th Georgia
26th Georgia Battalion
1st Georgia Battalion Sharpshooters

ARTILLERY BATTALION
Maj. Robert Martin
Howell's Georgia Battery, Capt. Evan P. Howell
Bledsoe's Missouri Battery, Capt. Hiram M. Bledsoe
Ferguson's South Carolina Battery, Capt. T. B. Ferguson

BRECKINRIDGE'S ARMY CORPS
Maj. Gen. John C. Breckinridge

CLEBURNE'S DIVISION
Maj. Gen. Patrick R. Cleburne

LIDDELL'S BRIGADE
Col. Daniel C. Govan
2nd/15th Arkansas
5th/13th Arkansas
6th/7th Arkansas
8th Arkansas
19th/24th Arkansas

SMITH'S BRIGADE
Brig. Gen. James A. Smith
6th/10th Texas
7th Texas
15th Texas (Dismounted) Cavalry
17th/18th/24th/25th Texas (Dismounted) Cavalry

POLK'S BRIGADE
Brig. Gen. Lucius E. Polk
1st Arkansas
3rd/5th Confederate
2nd Tennessee
35th/48th Tennessee

LOWREY'S BRIGADE
Brig. Gen. Mark P. Lowrey
16th Alabama
33rd Alabama
45th Alabama

32nd/45th Mississippi
15th Mississippi Battalion Sharpshooters

ARTILLERY BATTALION
Maj. T. R. Hotchkiss
Semple's Alabama Battery, Lieut. Richard W. Goldthwaite
Helena Arkansas Artillery (Calvert's), Lieut. Thomas J. Key
Warren Mississippi Battery (Swett's), Lieut. H. Shannon
Douglas's Texas Battery, Capt. James P. Douglas

STEWART'S DIVISION
Maj. Gen. Alexander P. Stewart

ADAM'S BRIGADE
Col. Randall L. Gibson
13th/20th Louisiana
16th/25th Louisiana
19th Louisiana
4th Louisiana Battalion
14th Louisiana Battalion Sharpshooters

STRAHL'S BRIGADE
Brig. Gen. Otho F. Strahl
4th/5th Tennessee
19th Tennessee
24th Tennessee
31st Tennessee
33rd Tennessee

CLAYTON'S BRIGADE
Col. J. T. Holtzclaw
18th Alabama
32nd/58th Alabama
36th Alabama
38th Alabama

STOVALL'S BRIGADE
Brig. Gen. Marcellus A. Stovall
40th Georgia
41st Georgia
42nd Georgia
43rd Georgia
52nd Georgia

ARTILLERY BATTALION
  Capt. Henry C. Semple
  Enfaula Alabama Artillery, Capt. McDonald Oliver
  Humphreys's Arkansas Battery, Lieut. John W. Rivers
  Dawson's Georgia Battery, Lieut. R. W. Anderson
  Stanford's Mississippi Battery, Capt. Thomas J. Stanford

BRECKINRIDGE'S DIVISION
  Brig. Gen. William B. Bate

LEWIS'S BRIGADE
  Brig. Gen. Joseph H. Lewis
  2nd Kentucky
  4th Kentucky
  5th Kentucky
  6th Kentucky
  9th Kentucky
  John H. Morgan's dismounted men

BATE'S BRIGADE
  Col. R. C. Tyler
  37th Georgia
  4th Georgia Battalion Sharpshooters
  10th Tennessee
  15th/37th Tennessee
  20th Tennessee
  30th Tennessee
  1st Tennessee Battalion Sharpshooters

FLORIDA BRIGADE
  Brig. Gen. Jessie J. Finley
  1st/3rd Florida
  4th Florida
  6th Florida
  7th Florida
  1st Florida (Dismounted) Cavalry

ARTILLERY BATTALION
  Capt. C. H. Slocomb
  Cobb's Kentucky Battery-Lieut. Frank P. Gracey
  5th Company, Washington Louisiana Artillery (Slocomb's)-
    Lieut. W. D. C. Vaught
  Mebane's Tennessee Battery-Capt. John W. Mebane

STEVENSON'S DIVISION
  Maj. Gen. Carter L. Stevenson

BROWN'S BRIGADE
  Brig. Gen. John C. Brown
  3rd Tennessee
  18th/26th Tennessee
  32nd Tennessee
  45th Tennessee/23rd Tennessee Battalion

CUMMING'S BRIGADE
  Brig. Gen. Alfred Cumming
  34th Georgia
  36th Georgia
  39th Georgia
  56th Georgia

PETTUS'S BRIGADE
  Brig. Gen. Edmund W. Pettus
  20th Alabama
  23rd Alabama
  30th Alabama
  31st Alabama
  46th Alabama

VAUGHN'S BRIGADE
  Brig. Gen. John C. Vaughn
  3rd Tennessee (Provisional Army)
  39th Tennessee
  43rd Tennessee
  59th Tennessee

ARTILLERY BATTALION
  Capt. William W. Carnes
  Cherokee Georgia Artillery, Capt. Max Van Den Corput
  Stephen Light Georgia Artillery, Capt. John B. Rowan
  Baxter's Tennessee Battery, Capt. Edmund D. Baxter
  Carnes Tennessee Battery, Lieut. L. Y. Marshall

WHEELER'S CAVALRY CORPS
  Maj. Gen. Joseph Wheeler

WHARTON'S DIVISION
  Maj. Gen. John A. Wharton

FIRST BRIGADE
  Col. Thomas Harrison
  3rd Arkansas
  65th North Carolina (6th Cavalry)
  8th Texas
  11th Texas

SECOND BRIGADE
  Brig. Gen. Henry B. Davidson
  1st Tennessee
  2nd Tennessee
  4th Tennessee
  6th Tennessee
  11th Tennessee

MARTIN'S DIVISION
  Maj. Gen. William T. Martin

FIRST BRIGADE
  Brig. Gen. John T. Morgan
  1st Alabama
  3rd Alabama
  4th Alabama (Russell's)
  Malone's (Alabama) Regiment
  51st Alabama

SECOND BRIGADE
  Col. J. J. Morrison
  1st Georgia
  2nd Georgia
  3rd Georgia
  4th Georgia
  6th Georgia

ARMSTRONG'S DIVISION
  Brig. Gen. Frank C. Armstrong

FIRST BRIGADE
  Brig. Gen. William Y. C. Humes
  4th Tennessee (Baxter Smith's)

5th Tennessee
8th Tennessee (Dibrell's)
9th Tennessee
10th Tennessee

SECOND BRIGADE
Col. C. H. Tyler
Clay's (Kentucky) Battalion
Edmundson's (Virginia) Battalion
Jessee's (Kentucky) Battalion
Johnson's (Kentucky) Battalion

KELLY'S DIVISION
Brig. Gen. John H. Kelly

FIRST BRIGADE
Col. William B. Wade
1st Confederate
3rd Confederate
8th Confederate
10th Confederate

SECOND BRIGADE
Col. J. Warren Grigsby
2nd Kentucky
3rd Kentucky
9th Kentucky
Allison's (Tennessee) Squadron
Hamilton's (Tennessee) Battalion
Rucker's Legion

ARTILLERY
Wiggins's Arkansas Battery, Capt. J. H. Wiggins
Huggins's Tennessee Battery, Capt. A. L. Huggins
Huwald's Tennessee Battery, Capt. Gustave A. Huwald
White's Tennessee Battery, Capt. B. F. White Jr.

RESERVE ARTILLERY
Maj. Felix H. Robertson
Lumsden's Alabama Battery-Lieut. Harvey H. Cribbs
Havis's Georgia Battery-Lieut. James R. Duncan
Jackson Georgia Artillery-Capt. Thomas L. Massenburg
Barret's Missouri Battery-Capt. Overton W. Barret

DETACHED

RODDY'S CAVALRY BRIGADE
  4th Alabama
  5th Alabama
  53rd Alabama
  Moreland's (Alabama) Battalion
  Ferrell's Georgia Battery, Capt. C. B. Ferrell

NOTES

Preface

1. Thomas L. Connelly, *Army of the Heartland: The Army of Tennessee, 1861–1862* (Baton Rouge: Louisiana State University Press, 1967), 3–10.

Chapter 1

1. For an overview of the Battle of Chickamauga and further detailed information about it, see Peter Cozzens, *This Terrible Sound: The Battle of Chickamauga* (Urbana: University of Illinois Press, 1992); David A. Powell, *The Chickamauga Campaign, A Mad Irregular Battle: From the Crossing of the Tennessee River Through the Second Day, August 22– September 19, 1863* (El Dorado Hills, CA: Savas Beatie, 2014), 227; David A. Powell, *The Chickamauga Campaign, Glory or the Grave: The Breakthrough, the Union Collapse, and the Defense of Horseshoe Ridge, September 20, 1863* (El Dorado Hills, CA: Savas Beatie, 2015), 59.

2. Cozzens, *This Terrible Sound*, 28–29, 299, 543n16; Powell, *Glory or the Grave*, 24–26.

3. Cozzens, *This Terrible Sound*, 363–65; For the latest scholarship on Wood's departure from the Union line around 11:05 a.m., see William Glenn Robertson, "A Tale of Two Orders: Chickamauga, September 20,

1863," in *Gateway to the Confederacy: New Perspectives on the Chickamauga and Chattanooga Campaigns, 1862–1863*, eds. Evan C. Jones and Wiley Sword (Baton Rouge: Louisiana State University Press, 2014), 142–55. Robertson maintains that there was no particular animosity between Wood and Rosecrans. Also according to Robertson, Maj. Gen. Alexander McCook reassured Wood that he would quickly replace the men Wood pulled out of line.

4. David A. Powell, *The Chickamauga Campaign: Barren Victory: The Retreat into Chattanooga, the Confederate Pursuit, and the Aftermath of the Battle, September 21 to October 20, 1863* (El Dorado Hills, CA: Savas Beatie , 2016), 10–16.

5. Ibid., 5; Cozzens, *This Terrible Sound*, 518.

6. Cozzens, *This Terrible Sound*, 519.

7. Ibid.; Wiley Sword, *Mountains Touched with Fire: Chattanooga Besieged, 1863* (New York: St. Martin's, 1995), 20; Alfred J. Vaughan Jr., *Personal Record of the Thirteenth Regiment, Tennessee Infantry, C.S.A.* (Memphis: S. C. Toof, 1897), 29; Marcus B. Toney, *The Privations of a Private: Bragg's Invasion of Kentucky* (Nashville, 1905), 60–61; W. M. Pollard, Diary, p. 6, Confederate Collection, Tennessee State Library and Archives, Nashville..

8. Cozzens, *This Terrible Sound*, 529; Powell, *Chickamauga Campaign*, 21–22.

9. Cozzens, *This Terrible Sound*, 528–29.

10. For a good description of the Confederate movements, see Powell, *Chickamauga Campaign*,, 58–78.

11. Thomas L. Connelly, *Autumn of Glory: The Army of Tennessee, 1862–1865* (Baton Rouge: Louisiana State University Press, 1971), 232–34; William R. Scaife, *The Campaign for Atlanta* (Cartersville, GA: Civil War Publications, 1993), 2–4.

12. Connelly, *Autumn of Glory*, 232–34.

13. Sword, *Mountains Touched with Fire*, 27.

14. US War Department, *The War of the Rebellion: A Compilation of the Official Records of the Union and Confederate Armies*, 128 vols. (Washington, DC: US Government Printing Office, 1880–1901), Series I (all citations are from series 1), hereafter cited as *OR*, vol. 31, pt. 2, 256.

15. Ibid., 133; Cozzens, *Shipwreck of Their Hopes*, 15; Connelly, *Autumn of Glory*, 232.

16. *OR*, vol. 31, pt. 2, 133.

17. Ibid.

18. Ibid.

19. Arthur Middleton Manigault, *A Carolinian Goes to War, the Civil War Narrative of Arthur Middleton Manigault: Brigadier General, C.S.A.*, ed. R. Lockwood Tower (Columbia: University of South Carolina Press, 1983), 131; John Hoffman, *The Confederate Collapse at the Battle of Missionary Ridge: The Reports of James Patton Anderson and His Brigade Commanders* (Dayton: Morningside, 1985), 57.

20. Peter Cozzens, *The Shipwreck of Their Hopes: The Battles for Chattanooga*, (Urbana: University of Illinois Press, 1992), 24–25; "Further reorganization of the army's command system was aimed at breaking up cliques—within corps, divisions, and brigades—of officers who were feeding one another's animosity toward Bragg." Quote in Steven E. Woodworth, *Jefferson Davis and His Generals: The Failure of Confederate Command in the West* (Lawrence: University Press of Kansas, 1990), 245; "By early November, Bragg had 'won' his struggle against the generals but at a high cost." Quote in Earl J. Hess, *Braxton Bragg: The Most Hated Man of the Confederacy* (Chapel Hill: University of North Carolina Press, 2016), 193.

21. Cozzens, *Shipwreck of Their Hopes*, 138.

22. Sword, *Mountains Touched with Fire*, 272–73; John Hoffman, *The Confederate Collapse at the Battle of Missionary Ridge*, 36–37.

23. John Hoffman, *The Confederate Collapse at the Battle of Missionary Ridge*, 36–37.

24. Author's in-depth discussion with Jim Ogden, chief historian, Chickamauga and Chattanooga National Military Park, March 15, 2015. James Lee McDonough, *Chattanooga—A Death Grip on the Confederacy* (Knoxville: University of Tennessee Press, 1984), 228.

25. *OR*, vol. 30, pt. 1, 142–43, 192–93; Sword, *Mountains Touched with Fire*, 15–16.

26. Cozzens, *Shipwreck of Their Hopes*, 18; Sword, *Mountains Touched with Fire*, 40–41.

27. Sword, *Mountains Touched with Fire*, 40–41.

28. Ibid.

29. Ibid.

30. Cozzens, *Shipwreck of Their Hopes*, 20.

31. Ibid., 103.

32. Ibid, 71–73. Ulysses S. Grant, *Memoirs of U. S. Grant* (1886; repr., Harrisburg, PA: Archive Society, 1997), 2:28. Although Grant takes the credit for establishing the "Cracker Line," in his *Memoirs,* it was Rosecrans who, following through on "Baldy" Smith's plan, initially ordered it to be established. This is covered in more detail in the critical decision made by Grant to open the "Cracker Line."

33. Cozzens, *Shipwreck of Their Hopes,* 143–44; Sword, *Mountains Touched with Fire,* 205–6.

34. Cozzens, *Shipwreck of Their Hopes,* 143–44; Sword, *Mountains Touched with Fire,* 238.

35. Sword, *Mountains Touched with Fire,* 135–37.

36. McDonough, *Chattanooga,* 35–36; Sword, *Mountains Touched with Fire,* 31–32; Cozzens, *Shipwreck of Their Hopes,* 23.

37. Cozzens, *Shipwreck of Their Hopes,* 23; Sword, *Mountains Touched with Fire,* 33.

38. *OR,* vol. 30, pt. 4, 744–45; Sword, *Mountains Touched with Fire,* 33–34.

39. Sword, *Mountains Touched with Fire,* 33; Connelly, *Army of the Heartland,* 243.40. Sword, *Mountains Touched with Fire,* 37.

41. Cozzens, *Shipwreck of Their Hopes,* 23–26.

42. Ibid., 23–29.

43. Sword, *Mountains Touched with Fire,* 69, 170.

44. Ibid., 43–44, 67–69.

45. Connelly, *Army of the Heartland,* 267. The number of soldiers available to Grant significantly favored his ability to break the semi-siege.

46. Ezra J. Warner, *Generals in Blue: Lives of the Union Commanders* (Baton Rouge: Louisiana State University Press, 1964), 196; Stanley F. Horn, *The Army of Tennessee* (Norman: University of Oklahoma Press, 1952), 160.

47. Grant, *Memoirs,* 2: 18; Cozzens, *Shipwreck of Their Hopes,* 4.

48. Cozzens, *Shipwreck of Their Hopes,* 51.

49. Ibid.

50. Ibid.

51. Cozzens, *Shipwreck of Their Hopes,* 4, 7; Sword, *Mountains Touched with Fire,* 51; Timothy B. Smith, *Shiloh: Conquer or Perish* (Knoxville: University of Tennessee Press, 2014), 6; Michael B. Ballard, *Vicksburg:*

The Campaign that Opened the Mississippi (Chapel Hill: University of North Carolina Press, 2004), 398; Abraham Lincoln, *Works of Abraham Lincoln*, edited by Roy P. Basler (New Brunswick, NJ: Rutgers University Press, 1959), 6:409; Sword, *Mountains Touched with Fire*, 51–52.

52. Cozzens, *Shipwreck of Their Hopes*, 100.

53. Ibid.

54. *OR*, vol. 30, pt. 1, 218; Carl Sandburg, *Abraham Lincoln* (New York: Dell, 1964), 2:434.

55. Cozzens, *Shipwreck of Their Hopes*, 4.

56. Ibid., 9.

57. John E. Clark, *Railroads in the Civil War: The Impact of Management on Victory and Defeat* (Baton Rouge: Louisiana State University Press, 2001), 7–8, 20 (map).

58. Cozzens, *Shipwreck of Their Hopes*, 17, 21–22; Grant, *Memoirs*, 2:28.

59. Cozzens, *Shipwreck of Their Hopes*, 46–47.

60. Ibid., 41–42.

61. Sword, *Mountains Touched with Fire*, 102.

62. Ibid., 51; Grant, *Memoirs*, 2:32.

63. Cozzens, *Shipwreck of Their Hopes*, 53–65, 78–100; Sword, *Mountains Touched with Fire*, 114–44.

64. Sword, *Mountains Touched with Fire*, 102.

65. Cozzens, *Shipwreck of Their Hopes*, 73.

66. Cozzens, *Shipwreck of Their Hopes*, 2, 45, 113; McDonough, *Chattanooga*, 54; Do not confuse the Confederate Army of Tennessee (state) with the Union Army of *the* Tennessee (River).

67. Cozzens, *Shipwreck of Their Hopes*, 4, 7, 112.

68. Ibid., 51, 108.

69. Ibid., 109.

70. Ibid., 107. However, Burnside himself was looking for reinforcements.

71. William T. Sherman, *Memoirs of General William T. Sherman in Two Volumes* (1875; repr., Harrisburg, PA: Archive Society, 1997), 1:357–58; Cozzens, *Shipwreck of Their Hopes*, 2, 47, 109, 122; Sword, *Mountains Touched with Fire*, 60; *OR*, vol. 31, pt. 1, 712–13, 716, 738.

72. *OR*, vol. 31, pt. 2, 64; *OR*, vol. 31, pt. 3, 179, 185; Sword, *Mountains Touched with Fire*, 160.

73. Sword, *Mountains Touched with Fire*, 157.

74. Ibid, 156.

75. Cozzens, *Shipwreck of Their Hopes*, 109; Sword, *Mountains Touched with Fire*, 60.

76. Sword, *Mountains Touched with Fire*, 30–33, 123–24.

77. Ibid., 124; Cozzens, *Shipwreck of Their Hopes*, 66, 68. The infighting concerned who would command Hood's division after he was wounded at Chickamauga—Brig. Gen. Evander McIvor Law or Brig. Gen. Micah Jenkins. In Sword, *Mountains Touched with* Fire, 131; Connelly, *Autumn of Glory*, 253–58.

78. Connelly, *Autumn of Glory*, 253–58.

79. Ibid.

80. Ibid.

81. Ibid.

82. Sword, *Mountains Touched with Fire*, 124.

83. Cozzens, *Shipwreck of Their Hopes*, 35.

84. Ibid., 66.

85. Ibid., 66–69.

86. Ibid., 70–100; Sword, *Mountains Touched with Fire*, 132–44.

87. Connelly, *Autumn of Glory*, 266–67.

88. Ibid., 258–59.

89. Ibid.

90. Sword, *Mountains Touched with Fire*, 69, 72.

91. Ibid., 69, 75–78.

92. Cozzens, *Shipwreck of Their Hopes*, 23–24.

93. Ibid., 103–4.

94. McDonough, *Chattanooga*, 98, 100.

95. Sword, *Mountains Touched with Fire*, 30, 64.

96. *OR*, vol. 52, pt. 2, 554; Sword, *Mountains Touched with Fire*, 76–77.

97. Sword, *Mountains Touched with Fire*, 77; Cozzens, *Shipwreck of Their Hopes*, 103.

98. National Park Service ranger and Chickamauga and Chattanooga National Military Park historian Lee White suggests Longstreet had this number of men. Sword, *Mountains Touched with Fire*, 78–79, maintains Longstreet had 15,000 and Burnside 23,000. Cozzens, *Shipwreck of Their Hopes*, 354, lists 18,500 with Longstreet and 12,000 with Burnside.

99. See previous note for numbers involved.

100. Author Matt Spruill compiled these numbers during research for his book *Storming the Heights: A Guide to the Battle of Chattanooga* (Knoxville: University of Tennessee Press, 2003).

101. Cozzens, *Shipwreck of Their Hopes*, 105; Connelly, *Autumn of Glory*, 267; McDonough, *Chattanooga*, 100.

Chapter 2

1. Cozzens, *Shipwreck of Their Hopes*, 124.

2. Ibid., 114; Sword, *Mountains Touched with Fire*, 156; *OR*, vol. 31, pt. 2, 571. Cozzens maintains that the reconnaissance occurred on November 15, while Sword and Sherman's report in the *Official Records* indicates that it was conducted on November 16.

3. Cozzens, *Shipwreck of Their Hopes*, 124. Thomas never lost a battle while in overall command.

4. McDonough, *Chattanooga*, 104; Sword, *Mountains Touched with Fire*, 104.

5. Cozzens, *Shipwreck of Their Hopes*, 108.

6. Ibid.

7. Ibid.

8. Ibid., 15, Connelly, *Autumn of Glory*, 273.

9. Grant, *Memoirs*, 2:52–60.

10. Ibid., 52–55; Cozzens, *Shipwreck of Their Hopes*, 124–25; Sword, *Mountains Touched with Fire*, 156–57, 190–198.

11. Cozzens, *Shipwreck of Their Hopes*, 151.

12. Sword, *Mountains Touched with Fire*, 205.

13. Cozzens, *Shipwreck of Their Hopes*, 114–15.

14. This alternate scenario which became reality will be discussed in the critical decision "Thomas's Troops Decide to Continue the Assault."

15. Cozzens, *Shipwreck of Their Hopes*, 125–27; *OR*, vol. 31, pt. 2, 32, 40.

16. Cozzens, *Shipwreck of Their Hopes*, 127.

17. Grant had only Eli Long's cavalry brigade present. Cozzens, *Shipwreck of Their Hopes*, 127, 405.

18. A reconnaissance in force is a deliberate combat operation designed to discover or test the enemy's strength, dispositions, and reactions, or to obtain other information. *Field Manual 3-90* (Washington, DC: Headquarters, Department of the Army, 4 July 2001), chapter 13.

19. Cozzens, *Shipwreck of Their Hopes*, 126–29; *OR*, vol. 31, pt. 2, 32–33.

20. Cozzens, *Shipwreck of Their Hopes*, 129–30.

21. Ibid., 135.

22. Ibid., 258.

23. Ibid., 141.

24. Ibid., 137.

25. Ibid., 135.

26. Hoffman, *Confederate Collapse*, 35, 57; Sword, *Mountains Touched with Fire*, 188; Cozzens, *Shipwreck of Their Hopes*, 196, 251–52;

27. Manigault, *A Carolinian Goes to War*, 134–35.

28. Ibid.; Cozzens, *Shipwreck of Their Hopes*, 252.

29. United States Army, *Dictionary of United States Army Terms* (Washington, DC: US Government Printing Office, 1983), 117.

30. Cozzens, *Shipwreck of Their Hopes*, 251–53.

31. See *OR*, vol. 20, pt. 1, 779, 897; vol. 23, pt. 1, 603; vol. 30, pt. 4, 557, 573; vol. 32, pt. 2, 476; vol. 38, pt. 3, 652; vol. 38, pt. 4, 746; vol. 45, pt. 2, 729–30; vol. 47, pt. 3, 873–74 for Green's progress through the war. Email with W. Glenn Robertson, October 20, 2015; George G. Kundahl, *Confederate Engineer, Training and Campaigning: John Morris Wampler*, Voices of the Civil War (Knoxville: University of Tennessee Press, 2000), 193–94; Manigault, *Carolinian Goes to War*, 134–35; Hoffman, *Confederate Collapse*, 14–15, 36, 41, 71; Sword, *Mountains Touched with Fire*, 188, 321; Cozzens, *Shipwreck of Their Hopes*, 251–52.

32. Cozzens, *Shipwreck of Their Hopes*, 250–51; Manigault, *A Carolinian Goes to War*, 134–35.

33. Manigault, *A Carolinian Goes to War*, 138.

34. This will be discussed in more detail in the critical decision "Thomas's Troops Decide to Continue the Assault."

35. Comment to author from National Park Service ranger Lee White, a historian at Chickamauga and Chattanooga National Military Park, spring 2017.

36. Manigault, *A Carolinian Goes to War*, 138.

Chapter 3

1. Cozzens, *Shipwreck of Their Hopes*, 150.

2. Ibid., 151–52.

3. Ibid., 152; Sword, *Mountains Touched with Fire*, 234.

4. Cozzens, *Shipwreck of Their Hopes*, 152; Sword, *Mountains Touched with Fire*, 234–35.

5. Sword, *Mountains Touched with Fire*, 235; Nathaniel Cheairs Hughes Jr., *General William J. Hardee: Old Reliable* (Baton Rouge: Louisiana State University Press, 1965), 171.

6. Cozzens, Shipwreck of Their Hopes, 152–54; Sword, *Mountains Touched with Fire*, 234–35.

7. *OR*, vol. 31, pt. 2, 678, 746; Sword, *Mountains Touched with Fire*, 236–37.

8. Sword, *Mountains Touched with Fire*, 234–35.

9. Connelly, *Autumn of Glory*, 275.

10. Ibid., 277; Hughes Jr., *General William J. Hardee*, 171.

11. Cozzens, *Shipwreck of Their Hopes*, 152.

12. Sunset time for November 24, 1863, Sunrise and Sunset Calculator, www.timeanddate.com/sun.

13. Cozzens, *Shipwreck of Their Hopes*, 157.

14. Ibid., 154.

15. Sword, *Mountains Touched with Fire*, 199–200.

16. Ibid.

17. Cozzens, *Shipwreck of Their Hopes*, 154–56.

18. Ibid., 200.

19. Ibid., 151.

20. Ibid.

21. Sword, *Mountains Touched with Fire*, 221.

22. Ibid. 163–64; Cozzens, *Shipwreck of Their Hopes*, 143–44.

23. Cozzens, *Shipwreck of Their Hopes,* 181.

24. Ibid., 192.

25. Ibid.; Sword, *Mountains Touched with Fire,* 221.

26. Sword, *Mountains Touched with Fire,* 221.

27. Ibid., 220.

28. Ibid., 221.

29. Ibid., 192–93; *OR,* vol. 31, pt. 2, 664, 678.

30. Sword, *Mountains Touched with Fire,* 221.

31. Ibid.

32. Ibid., 223; Cozzens, *Shipwreck of Their Hopes,* 169, 195–97.

33. Cozzens, *Shipwreck of Their Hopes,* 193–98; Sword, *Mountains Touched with Fire,* 229–30.

34. Cozzens, *Shipwreck of Their Hopes,* 192–93.

35. Ibid.

Chapter 4

1. Cozzens, *Shipwreck of Their Hopes,* 204–6.

2. Ibid., 205; Sword, *Mountains Touched with Fire,* 226.

3. Sword, *Mountains Touched with Fire,* 243, 248–49.

4. Cozzens, *Shipwreck of Their Hopes,* 204.

5. Sword, *Mountains Touched with Fire,* 248–49.

6. Ibid., 259.

7. Cozzens, *Shipwreck of Their Hopes,* 206–7.

8. Ibid., 207–8, 218.

9. Ibid., 207–16.

10. Sword, *Mountains Touched with Fire,* 232.

11. Cozzens, *Shipwreck of Their Hopes,* 241.

12. Ibid., 246; Grant, *Memoirs,* 2:77–78; *OR,* vol. 31, pt. 2, 34.

13. Grant, *Memoirs,* 2:78.

14. Cozzens, *Shipwreck of Their Hopes,* 246–47.

15. Ibid., 247.

16. Ibid.; Sword, *Mountains Touched with Fire,* 263.

17. Grant, *Memoirs*, 2: 78–79; Cozzens, *Shipwreck of Their Hopes*, 245–48. Per www.freedictionarydefinitions.com, a demonstration is "a show of military force or preparedness."

18. Cozzens, *Shipwreck of Their Hopes*, 262–72; Sword, *Mountains Touched with Fire*, 263–65.

19. Sword, *Mountains Touched with Fire*, 306–7.

20. Cozzens, *Shipwreck of Their Hopes*, 276–82.

21. Sword, *Mountains Touched with Fire*, 276–79.

22. Ibid.

23. Ibid., 278.

24. Connelly, *Autumn of Glory*, 271.

25. Cozzens, *Shipwreck of Their Hopes*, 282–88; McDonough, *Chattanooga*, 227–28.

26. Cozzens, *Shipwreck of Their Hopes*, 289–95.

27. Ibid., 276–81.

28. Ibid., 273.

Chapter 5

1. Cozzens, *Shipwreck of Their Hopes*, 343–54.

2. Ibid., 350–53.

3. Ibid., 364–65.

4. Ibid., 368; McDonough, *Chattanooga*, 220.

5. Horn, *Army of Tennessee*, 302; Sword, *Mountains Touched with Fire*, 334.

6. Horn, *Army of Tennessee*, 302; Sword, *Mountains Touched with Fire*, 334.

7. Horn, *Army of Tennessee*, 302; Sword, *Mountains Touched with Fire*, 334.

8. *OR*, vol. 31, pt. 2, 679; Cozzens, *Shipwreck of Their Hopes*, 368–69; McDonough, *Chattanooga*, 220–21; Sword, *Mountains Touched with Fire*, 334–35.

9. Cozzens, Shipwreck of Their Hopes, 368–69; Sword, *Mountains Touched with Fire*, 334–35.

10. Cozzens, *Shipwreck of Their Hopes*, 384.

11. Sword, *Mountains Touched with Fire*, 343; McDonough, *Chattanooga*, 225.

Chapter 6

1. Sword, *Mountains Touched with Fire*, 322; *OR*, vol. 31, pt. 2, 99–100.

2. Sword, *Mountains Touched with Fire*, 357; Cozzens, *Shipwreck of Their Hopes*, 391.

3. Sword, *Mountains Touched with Fire*, 321–22; *OR*, vol. 31, pt. 2, 12, 36, 88; Thomas L. Livermore, *Numbers and Losses in the Civil War in America: 1861–65* (Boston; Riverside, 1901) 106.

4. Sword, *Mountains Touched with Fire*, 352–54.

5. Grant, *Memoirs*, 2:114–15; Stephen Davis, *Atlanta Will Fall: Sherman, Joe Johnston and the Yankee Heavy Battalions* (Wilmington, DE: Scholarly Resources, 2001), 19; Richard M. McMurry, *Atlanta 1864: Last Chance for the Confederacy* (Lincoln: University of Nebraska Press, 2000), 1–2.

6. Grant, *Memoirs*, 2:130–32.

7. William R. Scaife, *The Campaign for Atlanta* (Cartersville, GA: Civil War Publications, 1993), 75–76, 120–21; Davis, *Atlanta Will Fall*, 102–17; McMurry, *Atlanta 1864*, 138–40, 175–76.

Appendix I

1. Peterson, *Confederate Combat Commander*, 131.

2. Ibid., 132.

3. *OR*, vol. 30, pt. 3, 812.

4. Connelly, *Autumn of Glory*, 247.

5. *OR*, vol. 30, pt. 4, 404.

6. *OR*, vol. 31, pt. 1, 221.

7. *OR*, vol. 31, pt. 2, 700.

8. Ibid., 678.

9. *OR*, vol. 31, pt. 1, 112–13.

10. Ibid., 231–33.

11. Ibid., 94.

12. Ibid., 86–87.

13. Ibid.

14. Grant, *Memoirs*, 2:28.

15. *OR*, vol. 31, pt. 3, 140.

16. Grant, *Memoirs*, 2:54–55.

17. Ibid., 62–64.

18. Manigault, *A Carolinian Goes to War*, 138–39.

19. Grant, *Memoirs*, 2:78–79.

20. Manigault, *A Carolinian Goes to War*, 136.

21. *OR*, vol. 31, pt. 3, 634.

22. Cozzens, *Shipwreck of Their Hopes*, 303. Other sources differ in Longstreet's actual numbers.

23. Manigault, *A Carolinian Goes to War*, 134–35.

24. *OR*, vol. 31, pt. 2, 746.

25. Ibid., 678.

26. United States Army, *Dictionary of United States Army Terms*, 117.

27. Ibid.

28. Ibid.

29. Ibid.

30. Cozzens, *Shipwreck of Their Hopes*, 246–47.

31. *OR*, vol. 31, pt. 2, 263.

32. Ibid., 574.

33. Ibid., 746.

34. Ibid., 754.

35. Cozzens, *Shipwreck of Their Hopes*, 384.

36. *OR*, vol. 31, pt. 2, 758.

BIBLIOGRAPHY

Primary Sources

Grant, Ulysses S. *Personal Memoirs of U. S. Grant in Two Volumes.* New York: Charles L. Webster & Company, 1886. Reprint. Harrisburg, PA: Archive Society, 1997.

Hoffmann, John, ed. *The Confederate Collapse at the Battle of Missionary Ridge: The Reports of James Patton Anderson and his Brigade Commanders.* Dayton: Morningside, 1985.

Lincoln, Abraham. *Works of Abraham Lincoln.* 8 vols. Edited by Roy P. Basler. New Brunswick, NJ: Rutgers University Press, 1959.

Longstreet, James. *From Manassas to Appomattox: Memories of the Civil War in America.* New York: Konecky & Konecky, 1992.

Pollard W. M. *Diary*, p. 6, Confederate Collection, Tennessee State Library and Archives, Nashville.

Sherman, William T. *Memoirs of General William T. Sherman in Two Volumes.* New York: D. Appleton , 1875. Reprint. Harrisburg, PA: Archive Society, 1997.

United States Army. *Dictionary of United States Army Terms.* Washington, DC: US Government Printing Office, 1983.

US War Department. *The War of the Rebellion: A Compilation of the Official Records of the Union and Confederate Armies.* 128 vols. Washington, DC: US Government Printing Office, 1880–1901.

Vaughan, Alfred J., Jr. *Personal Record of the Thirteenth Regiment, Tennessee Infantry, C.S.A. By Its Old Commander.* Memphis: S. C. Toof, 1897.

Secondary Sources

Ballard, Michael B. *Vicksburg: The Campaign that Opened the Mississippi.* Chapel Hill: University of North Carolina Press, 2004.

Black, Robert C. *The Railroads of the Confederacy.* Chapel Hill: University of North Carolina Press, 1998.

Boynton, Henry Van Ness. *The National Military Park: Chickamauga and Chattanooga, an Historical Guide, With Maps and Illustrations.* Cincinnati: Robert Clark, 1895.

Buell, Thomas B. *The Warrior Generals: Combat Leadership in the Civil War.* New York: Three Rivers, 1997.

Clark, John E. *Railroads in the Civil War: The Impact of Management on Victory and Defeat.* Baton Rouge: Louisiana State University Press, 2001.

Connelly, Thomas L. *Autumn of Glory: The Army of Tennessee, 1862–1865.* Baton Rouge: Louisiana State University Press, 1971.

Cozzens, Peter. *The Shipwreck of Their Hopes: The Battles for Chattanooga.* Urbana: University of Illinois Press, 1990.

———. *This Terrible Sound: The Battle of Chickamauga.* Urbana: University of Illinois Press, 1992.

Daniel, Larry J. *Soldiering in the Army of Tennessee: A Portrait of Life in a Confederate Army.* Chapel Hill: University of North Carolina Press, 1991.

Hess, Earl J. *Braxton Bragg: The Most Hated Man of the Confederacy.* Chapel Hill: University of North Carolina Press, 2016.

———. *Civil War Infantry Tactics: Training, Combat, and Small-Unit Effectiveness.* Baton Rouge: Louisiana State University Press, 2015.

Horn, Stanley F. *The Army of Tennessee.* 2nd ed. Norman: University of Oklahoma Press, 1952.

Hughes, Nathaniel Cheairs, Jr. *General William J. Hardee: Old Reliable.* Baton Rouge: Louisiana State University Press, 1965.

Jones, Evan C., and Wiley Sword, eds. *Gateway to the Confederacy: New Perspectives on the Chickamauga and Chattanooga Campaigns, 1862–1863.* Baton Rouge: Louisiana State University Press, 2014.

Kundahl, George G. *Confederate Engineer, Training and Campaigning: John Morris Wampler.* Voices of the Civil War. Knoxville: University of Tennessee Press, 2000.

Lewis, Lloyd. *Sherman, Fighting Prophet.* New York: Konecky & Konecky, 1932.

Losson, Christopher. *Tennessee's Forgotten Warriors: Frank Cheatham and His Confederate Division.* Knoxville: University of Tennessee Press, 1989.

Manigault, Arthur Middleton. *A Carolinian Goes to War: The Civil War Narrative of Arthur Middleton Manigault, Brigadier General, C.S.A.* Edited by R. Lockwood Tower. Columbia: University of South Carolina Press, 1983.

Marszalek, John E. *Sherman: A Soldier's Passion for Order.* New York: Vintage Books, 1994.

McDonough, James L. *Chattanooga—A Death Grip on the Confederacy.* Knoxville: University of Tennessee Press, 1984.

McMurry, Richard M. *Two Great Rebel Armies: An Essay in Confederate Military History.* Chapel Hill: University of North Carolina Press, 1989.

Peterson, Lawrence K. *Confederate Combat Commander: The Remarkable Life of Brigadier General Alfred Jefferson Vaughan Jr.* Knoxville: University of Tennessee Press, 2013.

Powell, David A. *The Chickamauga Campaign, A Mad Irregular Battle: From the Crossing of the Tennessee River Through the Second Day, August 22–September 19, 1863.* El Dorado Hills, CA: Savas Beatie, 2014.

———. *The Chickamauga Campaign, Barren Victory: The Retreat into Chattanooga, the Confederate Pursuit, and the Aftermath of the Battle, September 21 to October 20, 1863.* El Dorado Hills, CA: Savas Beatie, 2016.

———. *The Chickamauga Campaign, Glory or the Grave: The Breakthrough, the Union Collapse, and the Defense of Horseshoe Ridge, September 20, 1863.* El Dorado Hills, CA: Savas Beatie, 2015.

———. *Failure in the Saddle: Nathan Bedford Forrest, Joseph Wheeler, and the Confederate Cavalry in the Chickamauga Campaign.* New York: Savas Beatie, 2010.

———. *The Maps of Chickamauga: An Atlas of the Chickamauga Campaign, Including the Tullahoma Operations, June 22–September 23, 1863.* New York: Savas Beatie, 2009.

Sandburg, Carl. *Abraham Lincoln.* Vol. 2. New York: Dell, 1964.

Scaife, William R. *The Campaign for Atlanta.* Cartersville, GA: Civil War Publications, 1993.

Skinner, George W. *Pennsylvania at Chickamauga and Chattanooga.* Harrisburg, PA: William Stanley Ray, State Printer, 1901.

Smith, Timothy B. *Shiloh: Conquer or Perish.* Knoxville: University of Tennessee Press, 2014.

Spruill, Matt, ed. *Guide to the Battle of Chickamauga.* Lawrence: University Press of Kansas, 1993.

Spruill, Matt. *Storming the Heights, A Guide to the Battle of Chattanooga.* Knoxville: University of Tennessee Press, 2003.

Sword, Wiley. *Mountains Touched with Fire: Chattanooga Besieged, 1863.* New York: St. Martin's, 1995.

Symonds, Craig L. *Stonewall of the West: Patrick Cleburne & the Civil War.* Lawrence: University Press of Kansas, 1997.

Warner, Ezra J. *Generals in Blue: Lives of the Union Commanders.* Baton Rouge: Louisiana State University Press, 1964.

———. *Generals in Gray: Lives of the Confederate Commanders.* Baton Rouge: Louisiana State University Press, 1959.

Weber, Thomas. *The Northern Railroads in the Civil War, 1861–1865.* New York: Kings Crown, 1952. Reprint. Bloomington: Indiana University Press, 1999.

Wert, Jeffry D. *General James Longstreet: The Confederacy's Most Controversial Soldier.* New York: Simon & Schuster, 1993.

Woodworth, Steven E. *Decision in the Heartland: The Civil War in the West.* Westport, CT: Praeger, 2008.

———. *Jefferson Davis and His Generals: The Failure of Confederate Command in the West.* Lawrence: University Press of Kansas, 1990.

———. *Sherman.* New York: Palgrave McMillan, 2009.

———. *Six Armies in Tennessee: The Chickamauga and Chattanooga Campaigns.* Lincoln: University of Nebraska Press, 1998.

———. *This Great Struggle: America's Civil War.* Lanham, MD: Rowman & Littlefield, 2011.

Woodworth, Steven E., ed. *The Chickamauga Campaign.* Carbondale: Southern Illinois University Press, 2010.

Woodworth, Steven E., and Charles D. Grear, eds. *The Chattanooga Campaign.* Carbondale: Southern Illinois University Press, 2012.

INDEX